Adult Learner
Grammar Essentials

Plain English Explanations
+
Self-Study Exercises

Ashan R. Hampton

Cornerstone  Publishing
Arkansas

Published by Cornerstone Communications & Publishing, Little Rock, Arkansas.

For bulk orders, purchase orders or volume discounts, all booksellers, retailers or libraries should contact the publishing printer Lulu Enterprises Customer Service at 919-447-3244 or www.lulu.com.

Cover Design: Ashan R. Hampton / Cover photo: ©ThinkstockPhotos/Jupiterimages
Interior photos: © Can Stock Photo Inc. /focalpoint/blumer/moneca/scanrail

Website: www.arhampton.com

Library of Congress Control Number: 2019904739

ISBN-13: 978-0-359-69282-8

Hampton, Ashan R.
       Adult Learner Grammar Essentials /Ashan R. Hampton. — First Edition.
        pages cm
       Index included.
       ISBN-13: : 978-0-359-69282-8 (pbk)

1. English language—Grammar. 2. English language—Grammar—Problems, exercises, etc. 3. English language—Problems, exercises, etc. I. Ashan R. Hampton. Title.

Printed in the United States of America.
First Edition.

10 9 8 7 6 5 4 3 2 1

Online Grammar Classes
Additional Writing Resources

Beyond Basic Grammar

College Writing Essentials

Core Grammar Essentials

Proofreading Power

Smarty Pants Vocabulary Builders

Spelling Rules Refresher

Student Success Grammar

Find us online:

www.arhampton.com

Contents

Dedication

With great appreciation to Ms. Sara Lou Gifford at Philander Smith College and
Dr. E. Delores Stephens of Morehouse College. Thanks for my first teaching jobs and for
taking a chance on a young, temperamental English Instructor.

Some things never change.

To all of the *'challenging'* students that have ever met me in a classroom,
this, among other things, is what I was trying to teach you.

To all of my online students and editing clients,
thanks for validating and commending my skills.

To all English instructors everywhere...
oh, the poor, overworked, underpaid,
highly talented English teachers...
May God bless your life and show you
how to make more money!

About the Author

Ashan R. Hampton, graduated from the Donaghey Scholars Program at the University of Arkansas at Little Rock, and has been teaching English at colleges and universities since 1995, most notably at Morehouse College in Atlanta, Georgia. She is also a proud graduate of the *Donaghey Scholars Program* at the University of Arkansas at Little Rock under the direction of Dr. C. Earl Ramsey, Emeritus.

Through her published works, Ashan has contributed to the canons of Arkansas history. Ashan's original research project, *History of the Arkansas State Hospital 1859-1930*, was published in the *Pulaski County Historical Review* (1995), and continues to be cited by history scholars today. Her articles on notable African American Arkansans also appear in the *Encyclopedia of Arkansas History and Culture*.

With her doctoral studies on hold, Ashan has found success in online education. She produces and teaches original writing and grammar courses to global audiences. Ashan is the owner, principal editor and instructor for her consulting company, **Onyx Online Education & Training**, specializing in producing error-free documents and providing online writing classes.

Visit her website: **www.arhampton.com**.

15. When I tried to buy a birthday card for Michael, _____.

        a. the card shop was closed. ✓

        b. they were closed.

16. Melva smokes cigarettes even though _____.

        a. she knows it is bad for you.

        b. they are bad for her. ✓

17. Dexter owed a library fine, but he was sure he had brought _____.

        a. his books back on time. ✓

        b. them back on time.

18. When Jamal came looking for_____, we had already left.

        a. Karen and me

        b. Karen and I ✗

19. When we asked Haley to go to lunch with us, she said she _____ an hour ago.

        a. had ate

        b. had eaten ✓

20. "One of the cookies in this bag _____ a bite taken out of it," Jose complained.

        a. has

        b. have ✓

PRE-TEST ANSWERS

1. ~~After considering the job offer for some time~~, Jacob reluctantly decided ~~to accept it~~.

   The subject of the sentence is:

   a. job   b. offer   c. time   **d. Jacob**

   | Explanation: Subjects are not found in introductory clauses or prepositional phrases. |

2. ~~After considering the job offer for some time~~, Jacob reluctantly decided ~~to accept it~~.

   The verb of the sentence is:

   a. considering   b. offer   c. reluctantly   **d. decided**

   | Explanation: Verbs are not found in clauses, infinitive or prepositional phrases. |

3. ~~The bright yellow~~ paint ~~on the school bus~~ exactly matched Marcie's rain coat.

   The subject of the sentence is:

   a. paint   b. bus   c. Marcie   d. rain slicker

   | Explanation: The subject comes before the verb. The subject is not included in prepositional phrases. |

4. The bright yellow paint ~~on the school bus~~ exactly matched Marcie's raincoat.

   The verb of the sentence is:

   a. paint   **b. matched**   c. on   d. exactly

   | Explanation: Verbs are not found in clauses, infinitive or prepositional phrases. |

5. When Albert's supervisor asked where he was, his coworkers said that he _____ an hour ago.

   a. had went home   **b. had left**   c. gone home   d. leaved

   | Explanation: Option "b" correctly forms the past participle of the irregular verb "left." |

6. As she dashed through the parking lot toward the building, Chantal hoped that the exam had not already _____.

   a. begun   b. begin   c. began   d. beginned

   | Explanation: Option "a" correctly forms the past participle of the irregular verb "begun." |

7. The coins ~~in the jar on top of the microwave~~_____to be counted and rolled.

a. needs   **b. need**

> **Explanation:** *Coins* is a plural subject that needs a plural verb for proper agreement. Subjects are not found in prepositional phrases.

8. A bag ~~of carrots and half a tomato~~_____sitting ~~on the kitchen counter~~.

a. was   b. were

> **Explanation:** *Bag* is a singular subject that needs a singular verb (**was**).

9. One ~~of those sandwiches in the refrigerator~~_____for you.

a. are   **b. is**

> **Explanation:** *One* is a singular subject that needs a singular verb (**is**) for proper agreement.

10. ~~On a small table near the front of the classroom~~_____a dictionary, a thesaurus and a world globe.

a. sits   b. sits

> **Explanation:** Cross out all of the prepositional phrases. Do not get confused by sentence structure inversion. **Example:** A **dictionary, a thesaurus and a world globe sit** on a small table near the front of the classroom.

11. When we visited Bill's father at the plant, he was happy to give_____the grand tour.

a. Bill and I   **b. Bill and me**

> **Explanation:** Insert "me" in the blank to test for clarity. **Example:** He was happy to give **me** the grand tour.

12. Just between you and_____, Kristin was fired from her job.

a. I   **b. me**

> **Explanation:** Pronouns (**me or I**) that follow prepositions (**between**) take the objective case (me), ergo **between you and me**.

13. When Jana's parents came into town, _____tried to make them feel welcome.

a. she and me   **b. she and I**

> **Explanation:** Insert the pronouns (**she and I**) in the blank to test for clarity. **Example:** **I** tried to make them feel welcome. **She** tried to make them feel welcome.

14. We brought Jarod a dozen cookies while he was in the hospital, but _____.

    a. he was too sick to eat it.   **b. he was too sick to eat them.**

> Explanation: *Cookies* require a plural pronoun – **them**. The other pronouns are singular.

15. When I tried to buy a birthday card for Michael, _____.

    a. the card shop was closed.   b. they were closed.

> Explanation: This is the most specific and less confusing option.

16. Melva smokes cigarettes even though _____.

    a. she knows it is bad for you.   **b. they are bad for her.**

> Explanation: *Cigarettes* is a plural noun that needs a plural pronoun reference (**they**).

17. Dexter owed a library fine, but he was sure he had brought _____.

    a. his books back on time.   b. them back on time.

> Explanation: This option specifies *books*, which eliminates confusion or ambiguity. There is no reference for *them* in the sentence.

18. When Jamal came looking for_____, we had already left.

    a. Karen and me   b. Karen and I

> Explanation: Insert the pronouns (**me and I**) in the blank to test for clarity.

19. When we asked Haley to go to lunch with us, she said she _____ an hour ago.

    a. had ate   **b. had eaten**

> Explanation: Option "b" correctly forms the past participle of the irregular verb "**eaten.**"

20. "One ~~of the cookies in this bag~~ _____ a bite taken out of it," Jose complained.

    <u>a. has</u>   b. have

> Explanation: *One* is a singular subject that needs a singular verb **(has)** for proper agreement.

Chapter 1

PARTS OF SPEECH REVIEW

Adjective

[handwritten: Description word]

[handwritten: Person, place or thing]

[handwritten: a pronoun replaces a Noun]

An **adjective** is a description word that adds details to a noun or pronoun, such as color, size, number, or type. **Adjectives** that appear **before** the noun or pronoun they **modify** are called *attributive* adjectives. Adjectives enhance descriptions of people, places or things in very specific ways.

Adjectives often answer the questions:

- How many?

- What kind?

[handwritten: a red balloon — adjective — Noun]

> **Note:** **Modify** means to enhance or transform words with description.

Examples:

[handwritten: adjective (descriptive) Subject Noun]

- <u>Three</u> pages → How many?

- <u>Blue</u> folder → What kind? *[handwritten: adjective]*

- <u>Competent</u> supervisor → Adjective *[handwritten: Noun]*

- A <u>black, spandex</u> shirt → Multiple adjectives create vivid images for the reader.

- The <u>tall, gray, apartment</u> building on the corner of 6th and Louisiana St.

[handwritten: I saw her at the store. I saw Diane at the store. — Pronoun]

Notice the adjectives in the sentence below:

> Cynthia wore a **white**, **silk** wrap-dress and <u>**cherry red**</u> pumps with **gold** tips to the **cocktail** party.

Adjectives can also appear **after** <u>linking verbs.</u> When this happens, the adjective describes the subject or main noun that appears **before** the linking verb, as in the following examples.

a verb expresses condition, action or state of being.

ex:
- wrote
- escapes
- consumes

Linking Verbs

appear	look	prove	fall	were
become	sound	go	lay	been
grow	smell	stand	is	
remain	feel	work	am	
seem	taste	run	are	
get	continue	turn	was	

Examples:

subject

adverb modifies/describes a verb

S   LV   A
- Mrs. Gottbucks **is** generous with her money.
- The adjective **generous** comes after the linking verb **is** and describes **Mrs. Gottbucks**.

      S   LV   A
- Your **plan** to save the universe **sounds** interesting.
- The adjective **interesting** comes after the linking verb **sounds** and describes **plan**.

    S   LV   A
- Your **puppy** **looks** cute.
- The adjective **cute** comes after the linking verb **looks** and describes **puppy**.

Adverb

Adverbs usually describe or modify verbs. However, adverbs can also modify adjectives and other adverbs. One-word adverbs usually end in *–ly* (e.g. slowly).

Adverbs often answer the questions:
- How much?
- How often?
- To what degree?

Examples of Adverbs	Adverbs Modifying Adjectives and Other Adverbs
• walked **slowly**	• a **really** (adverb) cool (adjective) day
• typed **quickly**	• a **slightly** (adverb) **crooked** (adjective) nose
• Bob dresses **casually.**	• Silvia talks **very** (adverb) **loudly** (adverb).
• She speaks **well.**	• The weather is **extremely** (adverb) **hot** (adjective).

Antecedent

place, person or thing

An **antecedent** is a noun that a pronoun refers back to later in the sentence. The pronoun replaces the antecedent to avoid repetition. The antecedent is not always the subject of a sentence.

Examples:

- Teresa (antecedent) paid her (pronoun) dorm fee yesterday. *still Teresa*
- The football players (antecedent) experienced their (pronoun) first win today.
- Do you want a large cone (antecedent) or a small one (pronoun)?

Instead of repeating, "Do you want a large **cone** or a small **cone**? The pronoun "one" replaces the antecedent, "cone" to avoid repetition.

Article

Articles specify or point out particular places, people, things or ideas —in other words— nouns.

In English grammar, the following words are considered articles: **a, an, the.**

When to use the article "a"

- Use "**a**" when referring to a **single item**.
- Use "**a**" before nouns that begin with a **consonant letter** or **consonant sound**.
- **Consonants** consist of the alphabet letters: *Consonants*
  b, c, d, f, g, h, j, k, l, m, n, p, q, r, s, t, v, w, x, y, z
- Remember, "**a**" is considered an **indefinite article**, because it often refers to general items or approximate amounts. ↳ *Indefinite Article*

Examples of "a":

- a car
- a book
- a pencil

- a flute
- a kiwi
- a lamp

When to use the article "an"

- Use **"an"** when referring to a **single item.**

- Use **"an"** before nouns that begin with a **vowel letter** or **vowel sound.**

- **Vowels consist of the alphabet letters:**
  a, e, i, o, u and sometimes y

Examples of "an":

- an apple
- an igloo
- an odor

- an orange
- an idea
- an umpire

Exceptions to the articles "a & an"

- The "yoo" sound in the vowel letter **"u"** is also considered a **consonant** when it sounds like the consonant letter **"y."** Take for example the word *"unanimous."*

- Based on its pronunciation, the **"u"** in *"unanimous"* acts as a consonant, and is therefore paired with the article **"a." For example,** *"a unanimous decision."*

- When the letter **"u"** sounds like a vowel, it is paired with the article **"an."** For example, **"An ugly** couch blocked the doorway."

- In some words, as in the examples above, the consonant **SOUND** determines the article, not the actual letter.

Examples of Exceptions:

- a eulogy
- a historical novel
- a unicorn
- a uniform
- a unique situation

- a university
- an F.B.I. agent
- an honest man
- an hour ago
- a UAMS medical student

When to use the article "the"

- Use **"the"** when indicating or pointing out **specific items.**

- Use **"the"** when referring to multiple items, mass nouns or plural nouns.

Examples of "the":

- the air
- the melted butter
- the people
- the rocks

Clause

A **clause** is a group of related words that contains a subject and a verb. Clauses fit into two main categories: independent and dependent. An **independent clause** is a complete sentence. A **dependent clause** is an incomplete sentence, although it might also contain a subject and a verb.

Examples: <u>Subjects</u> are underlined once and <u>verbs</u> twice.

Independent Clauses (Complete Sentences)

- The <u>cable company</u> <u>provides</u> service to rural areas.
- The <u>firefighter</u> <u>carried</u> a little girl on his shoulders.
- <u>Summer school employees</u> <u>taught</u> many eager students.

Dependent Clauses (Incomplete Sentences)

- If <u>ten people</u> <u>complete</u> this survey
- After <u>Mark</u> <u>reads</u> this grammar book
- While <u>you</u> <u>live</u> in this house

Conjunction

A **conjunction** links one part of a sentence to another by connecting words, phrases and clauses.

- Conjunctions join two or more words or phrases.
- Conjunctions also join two or more complete sentences.

FANBOYS is a mnemonic that helps you remember these conjunctions.

Coordinating Conjunctions

for	F
and	A
nor	N
but	B
or	O
yet	Y
so	S

Examples of Conjunctions:

- Jack **and** Jill went up the hill.

- Terri enjoys walking, **but** not jogging.

- Eric knew I was right, **yet** he kept arguing.

Interjection

- An **interjection** is a word or phrase that expresses strong feeling or sudden emotion.

- An **interjection** is not a grammatical part of a sentence, which means the interjection can be removed without affecting the overall meaning or intent of the sentence.

Examples:

- **Ouch!** I stubbed my toe.   ~~Ouch!~~ I stubbed my toe.

- **Oh!** The water is too cold.   ~~Oh!~~ The water is too cold.

- **Fine!** I'll do it myself!   ~~Fine!~~ I'll do it myself!

Modifier

A **modifier** is a word, clause or phrase that describes or highlights the qualities of other words or parts of a sentence. **Adjectives** and **adverbs** are examples of modifiers.

Below, the **adjectives** appear in **bold** print and the **adverbs** in *italics*.

Example:

- The **handsome, sophisticated** professor walked *quickly* into the **cold,** *dimly lit* conference room.

Knowledge Check

1. A _____ is a group of related words with a subject and a verb.

2. A _____ connects sentences.

3. _____ can modify adjectives and verbs.

Answers on next page.

Answers: Knowledge Check

1. A <u>clause</u> is a group of related words with a subject and a verb.

2. A <u>conjunction</u> connects sentences.

3. <u>Adverbs</u> can modify adjectives and verbs.

Noun

A **noun** is a person, place, thing (object) or idea. Nouns appear in sentences as subjects, objects and complements. Common nouns refer to general items, but proper nouns identify specific people, places or things.

Examples:

- Person • priest, barber, teacher, librarian
- Place • New York City; Hot Springs, Arkansas
- Thing (Object) • stapler, computer, office chair
- Idea • justice, love, democracy, racial equality
- Common Nouns: • book, table, folder, teacher, calendar
- Proper Nouns: • President Barack Obama, *The Golden Girls*

Object

A **direct object** follows the verb and receives the action of the verb. Generally, an **indirect object** is the person or thing that receives the direct object.

Example:

We <u>purchased</u> a new <u>dishwasher</u>.
(Verb)   (Direct Object)

> **Finding the Object:**
> Identify the verb first then ask **what** or **whom.**

Examples of Objects:

The class <u>gave</u> **Professor Hampton** a <u>gift card</u> for her birthday.
(Verb)   (Indirect Object)   (Direct Object)

Phrase

Phrases consist of groups of related words that combine to express a single idea. Unlike clauses, phrases do not contain subjects or verbs.

Prepositional Phrase:
- Stop <u>at the count</u> <u>of ten</u>.

Infinitive Phrase:
- I have a bone <u>to pick</u> with you.

Participle Phrase:
- <u>Holding the dog by its collar</u>, the boy refused to let go.

Noun Phrase:
- <u>A tall, dark-haired man</u> entered the conference room.

Gerund Phrase:
- <u>Using profane language</u> is not allowed here.

Verb Phrase:
- She <u>could have been watching</u> him from the café across the street.

Knowledge Check

1. A _____ is a person, place or thing.

2. _____ receive the action of the verb.

3. _____ express strong emotions.

Answers on next page.

Answers: Knowledge Check

1. A <u>noun</u> is a person, place or thing.

2. <u>Objects (Direct)</u> receive the action of the verb.

3. <u>Interjections</u> express strong emotions.

Preposition

Prepositions show the relationship between subjects and objects by describing location or position. A preposition must be followed by an object (noun or pronoun), which is called the **object of the preposition**. The combination of the preposition and its object forms a **prepositional phrase**. Prepositional phrases provide a sense of clarity and completeness to the sentence.

Common Prepositions

about	before	from	over	under
above	behind	in	past	underneath
after	below	inside	regarding	unlike
against	beside	into	round	up
along	between	near	since	upon
alongside	by	of	than	until
among	down	off	through	unto
around	during	on	throughout	with
at	except	out	to	within
because	for	outside	toward	without

Examples of Prepositions:

- Long ago, farmers smoked bacon **by hanging it** **in their chimneys**.

- Little Rock is the capital **of Arkansas**.

- X-rays can detect cracks **in metal**.

Pronoun

A **pronoun** replaces a noun, another pronoun or noun phrase. The pronoun substitution does not change the structure or meaning of the sentence.

Examples:

- I saw **Diane** yesterday at the grocery store.

Diane = Noun

- I saw **her** (Diane) yesterday at the grocery store.

  Her = Pronoun

Needless Pronoun Repetition

- **Donna** entered the room, but **Donna** did not say anything to us.
  (Noun)   (Noun)

Correction: Needless Pronoun Repetition

- **Donna** entered the room, but <u>she</u> did not say anything to us.
  (Noun)   (Pronoun)

Common Pronouns:

Subject Pronouns	I	he	she	we	they	who	you	it
Object Pronouns	me	him	her	us	them	whom	you	it
Possessive Pronouns	my	his	her	our	their	whose	your	its
	mine		hers	ours	theirs		yours	

Sentence

A **sentence** is a group of words that includes a <u>subject</u> and a <u>verb</u> (predicate). A sentence expresses a complete thought.

Examples of Sentences:

- The night <u>janitor</u> <u>emptied</u> the trashcans and set the alarm.

- <u>Ahnna and Ashley</u> frequently <u>shop</u> at the mall.

- <u>Ramona</u> <u>sings</u> in the church choir.

Subject

A **subject** is a noun, pronoun or noun phrase that performs the action of the verb. The action of the sentence revolves around the subject. The subject usually takes the form of a person, place, thing or idea that explains what or whom the sentence is about.

Examples of Subjects:

- The financial **analyst** examined the report.
- **Zumba** is the reigning fitness craze of the day.

Verb

A **verb** expresses action, condition or state of being. The verb tells what is happening within a sentence. Verbs also give a sense of time and are written in the **past, present** or **future tense.** Technically, only two verb tenses exist in the English language: past and present. Although verbs and time clue words are combined to express future tense, standard English does not recognize a separate future tense for verbs as in Latin.

Examples of Verbs:

- Donald **wrote** books for students and educators.
- Justice **escapes** the poor and **consumes** the rich.
- Kim **will travel** to Puerto Rico for her birthday.

Present Tense:

- The teacher **opens** the door for the principal.

Remember:
There is no direct future tense in the English language.

Past Tense:

- Trisha **walked** around the parking lot during a break at work to get more exercise.

Expression of Future:

- Todd **will speak** at the college recruitment fair **tomorrow**.

EXERCISE 1
GRAMMAR TERMS

Directions: Write the correct grammar term for each definition below.

1. _____ Names a person, place, thing or idea.

2. _____ Describes or modifies a verb or adjective.

3. _____ Replaces a noun or noun phrase.

4. _____ Suggests action or state of being.

5. _____ Includes the words *I, you, we, he* and *she*.

6. _____ Connects words, phrases and clauses.

7. _____ Specifies or points out particular nouns.

8. _____ Expresses strong feelings.

9. _____ Describes location or position.

10. _____ Receives the action of the verb.

Answers on page 145.

EXERCISE 2

GRAMMAR TERMS

Directions: For each **bold highlighted word** in the sentences below, write the part of speech (grammar term) it represents in the blank.

Example: **Preposition**   Teresa stopped **by** the store **on** the way home.

1. _____ **Good** sunglasses need not be expensive.

2. _____ Melissa **is** too short to get a good view of the stage.

3. _____ Using skim **milk** on cereal lowers the total fat content.

4. _____ Ralph **rarely** balances his checkbook.

5. _____ Marcie walks frequently, **but** she rarely drives.

6. _____ Dorothy never opens **her** junk mail.

7. _____ Cortisone **reduces** inflammation.

8. _____ **Oh**, Jan, your plastic rain hat melted in the dryer.

9. _____ Julie made **a** braided rug out of discarded clothes.

10. _____ The eye **of** the law is narrow and myopic.

Answers on page 145.

EXERCISE 3

GRAMMAR TERMS

Directions: For each **bold highlighted word** in the sentences below, write the part of speech (grammar term) it represents in the blank.

Example: **Verb** Marlow **graduated** college in May.

1. _____ Never **peel** the bark from a birch tree.

2. _____ Fasten your seat belt for the **take-off**.

3. _____ Dad is using his new **power** saw.

4. _____ The crew rowed **hard** at the finish.

5. _____ **Nobody** in the room could identify the wallet.

6. _____ **Before** the telecast, we were all nervous.

7. _____ Hot water revives **cut** flowers.

8. _____ Each year the firemen **stage** a water duel.

9. _____ The **suspect** was wearing a tan jacket.

10. _____ **Outside** the embassy, a crowd gathered.

Answers on page 145.

EXERCISE 4
ARTICLES

Directions: Choose the correct **article** for each sentence and write it in the blank.
Articles: a   an   the

1. Jill makes it _____ habit to buy clothes on sale.

2. To tell _____ truth, free checking accounts are hardly ever free of bank charges.

3. Sheila always wears _____ uniform to work.

4. Corey makes ten dollars _____ hour at his part-time job.

5. Major changes have occurred in _____ educational field.

6. Charles stores extra cash in _____ empty cereal box.

7. Clutter can make _____ room seem smaller.

8. Taking a hot bath is _____ good way to relax.

9. Dr. Taylor predicts _____ extinction of the whooping crane.

10. Most people believe that _____ Statue of Liberty is very precious.

Answers on page 145.

Chapter 2

BASIC SENTENCE STRUCTURE

What is a Sentence?

A **sentence** is a group of words that includes a <u>subject</u> and a <u>verb</u> (**predicate**). A sentence expresses a complete thought.

In basic sentence structure, the subject comes first followed by the verb. Additional **complements**, (phrases or descriptions that complete or enhance the sentence), usually follow the verb.

Basic Sentence Structure

<u>Subject</u> + <u>Verb</u> + Object/Complement/Phrase/Clause (completion of the statement) = **a complete sentence.**

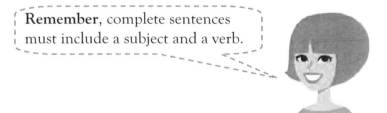

Remember, complete sentences must include a subject and a verb.

Grammar Term Reminders:

Subject:	A noun, pronoun or noun phrase that performs the action of the verb. Explains what or whom the sentence is about.
Verb:	A word or phrase that expresses action, condition or state of being. Explains what happened.

Simple Subject

The **simple subject** consists of one word. Adjectives or other modifiers are not included in the simple subject. The <u>subject</u> of a sentence is commonly identified with a single underline.

Example:

- The sky-blue <u>umbrella</u> broke in the windy rainstorm.

In this example, the adjective, *sky-blue,* is not included in the simple subject, <u>umbrella</u>.

Subject: Understood You

Sometimes the subject of the sentence is understood, but not directly stated. **Imperative statements** or command sentences contain an implied **"you"** as the subject.

Examples of Imperative Sentences:

- Close the door.

- Put the sandwich on a paper towel.

Who should close the door? **You.** Who should put the sandwich on a paper towel? **You!**

- **(You)** Close the door.

- **(You)** Put the sandwich on a paper towel.

Complete Subject

The complete subject includes the simple subject and all the words that come before the verb.

Example:

- <u>The sky-blue umbrella</u> broke in the windy rainstorm.

In this example, the entire phrase, *the sky-blue umbrella*, consists of the complete subject.

Simple Verb

The simple verb usually consists of one root action word written in the past or present tense.

Example:

- The sky-blue umbrella <u>broke</u> in the windy rainstorm.

In this example, the word, *broke* is the simple verb.

- Clara <u>will speak</u> at the faculty meeting.

The helping verb, *will*, combines with the main action verb, *speak*, to make one verb phrase that expresses future tense. In the second example, notice that the sentence does not make sense without the helping verb, *will*.

- Clara <u>**will speak**</u> at the faculty meeting.

- Clara <u>**speak**</u> at the faculty meeting.

The Predicate

The predicate includes the simple verb and all the words that come after the verb.

Example:

- The sky-blue umbrella <u>**broke in the windy rainstorm**</u>.

In this example, the phrase, ***broke in the windy rainstorm***, is called the predicate. Notice that the predicate starts with the verb (**broke**) and includes all the other words that follow the verb.

- A **complete sentence** contains a **subject** and a **predicate**.

- The **predicate** begins with the first verb in a sentence and continues to the end of the sentence.

Types of Sentences

Sentences are divided into four main categories:

- Simple
- Compound
- Complex
- Compound-Complex

Simple Sentence

Like all complete sentences, a **simple sentence** contains a subject and a predicate. A simple sentence is composed of only one independent clause. Basically, a simple sentence contains one subject-predicate unit and no dependent clauses.

One Subject, One Verb

• <u>Craig</u> <u>plays</u> the alto saxophone in a community jazz band.

<u>Complete Subject</u>   =   <u>Craig</u>

<u>Complete Predicate</u> = <u>plays</u> the alto saxophone in a community jazz band.

Two Subjects, One Verb

• <u>**The textbook and lectures confused**</u> the business students.

<u>Complete Subject</u>   =   The textbook and lectures

<u>Complete Predicate</u> =   <u>confused</u> the business students.

One Subject, Two Verbs

• The old <u>**car**</u> <u>**sputtered**</u> and <u>**blew**</u> smoke from the tailpipe at the stoplight.

<u>Complete Subject</u>   =   The old <u>**car**</u>

<u>Complete Predicate</u> = <u>**sputtered**</u> and <u>**blew**</u> smoke from the tailpipe at the stoplight.

Two Subjects, Two Verbs

• <u>**Melanie and Tim drove**</u> all night to attend the Janet Jackson concert in Memphis, but <u>**slept**</u> through the opening act.

<u>Complete Subject</u>   =   <u>**Melanie and Tim**</u>

<u>Complete Predicate</u> =   <u>**drove**</u> all night to attend the Janet Jackson concert in Memphis, but <u>**slept**</u> through the opening act.

Compound Sentence

A **compound sentence** consists of two complete sentences (two independent clauses) joined by a coordinating conjunction.

Compound Sentence 1:

Carl owns a large collection of comic books, **but** he rarely reads them.

{Sentence 1}	{Sentence 2}
Carl owns a large collection of comic books.	He rarely reads them.

Compound Sentence 2:

Darren has visited The Alamo three times, **and** he is still fascinated by the monument.

{Sentence 1}	{Sentence 2}
Darren has visited The Alamo three times.	He is still fascinated by the monument.

Complex Sentence

A **complex sentence** contains one complete sentence (independent clause) and one or more dependent clauses. Even if the clauses are removed, one complete sentence still remains.

Complex Sentence 1:

When Tricia received the estimate for repairs, she decided to sell the car.

{Dependent Clause}	{Sentence 1}
~~When Tricia received the estimate for repairs,~~	She decided to sell the car.

Complex Sentence 2 :

After the wedding coordinator released the doves, which did not fly very far into the air, the bride and groom laughed at the attempt and headed to the reception.

{Dependent Clause 1}	{Dependent Clause 2}
After the wedding coordinator released the doves,	which did not fly very far into the air

{Complete Sentence 1}
The bride and groom laughed at the attempt and headed to the reception.

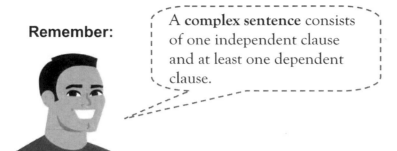

Remember:

A **complex sentence** consists of one independent clause and at least one dependent clause.

Knowledge Check

1. A _____ includes one subject and one verb.

2. A _____ includes a simple verb and all the words that follow.

3. A _____ contains two independent clauses.

Answers on next page.

Subordinating Conjunctions

Dependent clauses often begin with subordinating conjunctions. **Subordinating conjunctions** join a dependent clause to an independent clause (complete sentence). In the case of subordination, one clause is more important than the other. Since the independent clause is more important, the dependent clause is under or subordinate to the main part of the sentence, which is the independent clause.

Subordinating Conjunctions:

after	till
although	unless
as	until
because	when
before	whenever
if	wherever
since	while
than	why

Relative pronouns also function as **subordinating conjunctions** that usually appear in the middle or toward the end of a sentence.

Relative Pronouns (Subordinating Conjunctions):

who	which
whom	what
whose	that

1. A <u>simple sentence</u> includes one subject and one verb.

2. A <u>predicate</u> includes a simple verb and all the words that follow.

3. A <u>compound sentence</u> contains two independent clauses.

Compound-Complex Sentence

A **compound-complex sentence** contains <u>two complete sentences</u> (independent clauses) and at least one dependent clause. Deleting the dependent clauses does not affect the two complete sentences.

Compound-Complex Sentence 1:

- Before the game started, Freddy cooked buffalo wings and Tanisha poured drinks for everybody.

{Dependent Clause}	{Sentence 1}	{Sentence 2}
Before the game started,	Freddy cooked buffalo wings.	Tanisha poured drinks for everybody.

Compound-Complex Sentence 2:

- Timothy invited Amasa Hines to play at Riverfest, which was scheduled during Memorial Day weekend, but the band had already accepted gigs in Memphis.

{Sentence 1}

Timothy invited Amasa Hines to play at Riverfest.

{Dependent Clause}

which was scheduled during Memorial Day weekend

{Sentence 2}

The band had already accepted gigs in Memphis.

Putting it all together

Example Sentence (Complex):

- In less than a week, the state education **committee** **completed** the work and **submitted** its report to the governor a month before the deadline.

In less than a week	dependent clause
the	article
state, education	adjectives
committee	subject (noun)
completed	verb 1
the work	direct object
and	coordinating conjunction
submitted	verb 2
its	possessive (object) pronoun
report	direct object
to the governor	prepositional phrase
a	article
month	noun
before the deadline	prepositional phrase

EXERCISE 1
Types of Sentences

Directions: Write whether the following sentences are **simple**, **complex**, **compound** or **compound-complex** in the space provided.

Example: <u>**Simple**</u>   Girls are made of sugar and spice and everything nice.

1. _____ Facts are sometimes changeable.

2. _____ Ashan's last novel, which we will discuss later, raises interesting questions about the origins of her inspiration.

3. _____ Rita and Charles have never traveled more than one hundred miles from home, and they have never stayed away for more than two days.

4. _____ The most interesting of Widow Bush's gifts to the museum was a large collection of cotillion gowns.

5. _____ The Anthony brothers opened a music studio in Arkansas, but soon after, David abandoned the business to become a music teacher.

6. _____ In ancient Egypt, general surgery was quite common, and this fact is depicted by archeological surveys.

7. _____ Kings were once thought to have the miraculous ability to cure disease by the laying on of hands.

8. _____ We tend to love those who admire us, but we do not always love those whom we admire.

9. _____ Sharese has been to Disneyland five times and she is still fascinated by its grandeur.

10. _____ In his religious and inspirational writings, Thomas D. Jakes motivates the masses.

Answers on page 146.

EXERCISE 2
Identifying Clauses

Directions: Underline the **dependent clauses.**

Example: The adjuncts hoped <u>**that the hiring freeze would end soon**</u>.

1. Peter was a disciple who denied Jesus three times.

2. The NAACP, which was founded in 1910, accomplished a great deal in the struggle for civil rights.

3. Presidential candidates must strike while the iron is hot.

4. If wishes were horses, beggars would ride.

5. Since Mr. Johns, the best principal in the district, retired, many teachers do not feel secure or supported in their classrooms.

6. Jesse and Jeremy always get into trouble whenever their cousin Rob comes to town.

7. When planning a garden, you must consider the annual temperature range in your area.

8. Mozart, who was a musical genius and a child prodigy, died young.

9. Because love is not a requirement for marriage, many marriages end in divorce.

10. After lunch is served, students prepare for recess.

Answers on page 146.

EXERCISE 3
Identifying Subjects

Directions: Underline the **complete subject** in each sentence.
Example: <u>**Pastor Christian and his wife**</u> spearheaded the school supply drive.

1. Where is the school district headed with this interim superintendent?

2. Heavy rains washed out all Halloween activities in the neighborhood.

3. Jane stood in front of her desk.

4. On his way to work, Todd stopped for coffee.

5. Please share your story with us.

6. Craig and Karen got married on Thanksgiving Day.

7. Ahnna and her co-workers decorated the office for National Boss's Day.

8. Kevin and Kandis threw themselves an old school birthday party.

9. Throw the dirty clothes in the hamper.

10. The trees burst into color with the arrival of autumn leaves.

Answers on page 146.

EXERCISE 4
Subjects and Predicates

Directions: **Circle** the simple **subject** and **underline** the **complete predicate**.

Example: (Rent) **is a large item in our budget**.

1. You should bring a change of clothes to the beach.

2. Shanda always stretches before going on her daily run.

3. A box of cookies is in the cupboard behind the peanut butter.

4. One of Josephine's contact lenses fell out of her eye.

5. A mystery admirer from Ian's office sent a bouquet of flowers.

6. I should have taken more writing courses before going to graduate school.

7. Miguel can tell the difference between a male and a female parrot.

8. Bram Stoker is best known for his novel, *Dracula*.

9. Your tickets will be sent to you by the first week of November.

10. One of our subscribers wrote a letter of complaint about the magazine.

Answers on page 147.

Chapter 3

SENTENCE FRAGMENTS

What is a Fragment?

A **sentence fragment** is an incomplete clause that does not express a complete thought. Although a fragment might contain a subject and a verb, the sentence is still missing some important information. The missing part makes the sentence sound unfinished or strange.

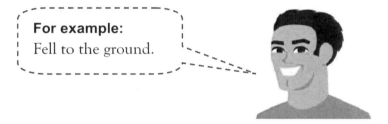

For example:
Fell to the ground.

In the above example, more information is required to make the action of the sentence clear to the reader. **What fell to the ground?** Who or what is the subject? If someone spoke this sentence to you and stopped talking, you would immediately start asking questions as a natural need for clarity.

Since fragments are unclear, you must fill in the missing information to correct the sentence and to relieve the reader's frustration.

Correction:

- <u>Ashan's corndog</u> fell to the ground.

Even Better:

- **Ashan's footlong corndog,** drenched in mustard, rolled off the picnic table at the state fair and fell to the ground.

Fragments: Missing Subjects

Sometimes fragments occur when subjects are missing from sentences.

Example:

- Communicated the latest sales figures.

Who? Where is the <u>subject</u>?

Correction:
- <u>Britt</u> communicated the latest sales figures.

Fragments: Missing Verbs

Sometimes fragments occur when verbs are missing from sentences.

Example:
- All the students in the classroom.

   Did what? Where is the verb?

Correction:
- All the students in the classroom **<u>played</u>** board games.

Fragments: Incomplete Verbs

Sometimes fragments occur when helping verbs are missing from sentences. When the helping verb or auxiliary is missing from the verb phrase, the resulting partial sentence sounds odd or unfinished.

Example:
- Psychics taking grieving widows' money.

In this example, **"taking"** is a participle verb that needs to become a past or present participle verb phrase. Either the word **"were"** or **"are"** should be inserted before **"taking"** to complete the sentence.

Correction:
- Psychics **<u>were taking</u>** grieving widows' money.    Past Participle

- Psychics **<u>are taking</u>** grieving widows' money.   Present Participle

Fragments: Infinitive and Prepositional Phrases

Sometimes fragments occur when infinitive or prepositional phrases are included in the sentence. These phrases will never contain the true subject or verb of the sentence. Although **infinitive phrases** contain a verb, it is not the main verb of the sentence. On the other hand, although **prepositional phrases** include nouns (the object of the preposition), the true subject of the sentence is never found in a prepositional phrase. Infinitives and prepositions make a sentence seem to have a subject and verb when it really does not, which creates a fragment.

Example:

- To control the flow of air in the room.

Before we get to the correction for this sentence, let's identify the infinitive and prepositional phrases first.

- **Infinitive:** to control
- **Infinitive phrase:** to control the flow
- **Prepositional Phrase 1:** of air
- **Prepositional Phrase 2:** in the room

Now that we have identified the infinitive and prepositional phrases, let's go back and correct the original example.

Example:

- To control the flow of air in the room.

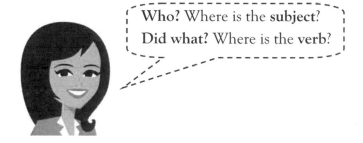

Who? Where is the **subject**?
Did what? Where is the **verb**?

Correction:

- <u>Erma</u> <u>lowered</u> the thermostat to control the flow of air in the room.

In order to transform this collection of infinitive and prepositional phrases into a complete sentence, we had to add a subject, a verb and a direct object.

- Erma = <u>subject</u>
- lowered = <u>verb</u>
- the thermostat = **direct object**

Fragments: Gerund Phrases

Gerunds appear to be verbs that end with the suffix *-ing*. However, gerunds actually function as nouns, **usually the subject of a sentence**, as subject complements or objects. The confusion that gerunds present can lead to sentence fragments. Gerund phrases often seem to include elements of a complete sentence when they are indeed fragmented.

Example:

- Refusing to accept his loss.

In this sentence, **"refusing"** would typically be a verb, but in this example, it is not functioning as a true verb, but as a gerund. Gerunds often appear at the beginning of sentences, and in some cases function as the subject of a sentence. **Remember, gerund phrases and infinitive phrases do not constitute the main verb or the main action of a sentence**.

Remember, **gerunds** and **infinitives** do not function as main verbs.

Correction:

- **Refusing to accept his loss** caused Bryan to quit the track team.

Remember, the subject comes **before** the verb. In this example, the gerund phrase, *refusing to accept his loss*, are the only words preceding the verb <u>caused</u>. Therefore, the gerund phrase is the subject of this sentence. *Caused* what? To quit the track team. *Who* quit? Bryan.

- Refusing to accept his loss = <u>subject</u> (gerund phrase)
- caused = <u>verb</u>
- Bryan = **indirect object**
- to quit the track team = **direct object** (infinitive phrase)

Tips for Fixing Fragments

1. Read your writing aloud. Generally, it is easier to **hear** missing words than to **see** them on a printed page or computer screen.

2. Find the true subject of the sentence.

3. Find the true verb.

Knowledge Check

1. A _____ is an incomplete thought.

2. A _____ appears to be a verb, but is actually a noun (phrase).

3. _____ and _____ are not main verbs.

Answers at bottom of page.

1. fragment 2. gerund 3. gerunds and infinitives

EXERCISE 1
Sentence Fragments

Directions: Decide if each sentence is a **fragment** or a **complete sentence. Circle the correct answer.**

1. Advised against buying extra rustproofing for the new car.

    a. Complete Sentence

    b. Fragment

2. All smoking in the building will be prohibited after July first.

    a. Complete Sentence

    b. Fragment

3. Each year plants trees near the neighborhood schools.

    a. Complete Sentence

    b. Fragment

4. Karen is saving money to buy a new air conditioner.

    a. Complete Sentence

    b. Fragment

5. Gives the user a painful shock.

    a. Complete Sentence

    b. Fragment

6. Did not understand the side effects of the medication he took.

    a. Complete Sentence

    b. Fragment

7. The clown made the children at the party laugh.

        a. Complete Sentence

        b. Fragment

8. A minor must consult her parents before receiving birth control.

        a. Complete Sentence

        b. Fragment

9. Rolls back more than fifty odometers every day.

        a. Complete Sentence

        b. Fragment

10. To get rid of the mice.

        a. Complete Sentence

        b. Fragment

Answers on page 147.

EXERCISE 2
Sentence Fragments

> **Directions:** Decide if each sentence is a **fragment** or a **complete sentence**. **Circle the correct answer.**

1. The movie begins at three o'clock in the afternoon.

      a. Complete Sentence

      b. Fragment

2. The Fitzpatricks are actually installing.

      a. Complete Sentence

      b. Fragment

3. The pricing structure leads to higher rates.

      a. Complete Sentence

      b. Fragment

4. A frazzled reporter ran into the newspaper office.

      a. Complete Sentence

      b. Fragment

5. Directly under a high voltage power line.

      a. Complete Sentence

      b. Fragment

6. Doughnuts labeled "lite" are hardly diet foods.

      a. Complete Sentence

      b. Fragment

7. A person who is so obviously self-disciplined.

    a. Complete Sentence

    b. Fragment

8. Burglars prefer quiet ways of entering a home, such as picking a lock.

    a. Complete Sentence

    b. Fragment

9. Since Regina forgot to charge the flashlight.

    a. Complete Sentence

    b. Fragment

10. Food cooked on a gas grill tastes the same as food cooked on a charcoal grill.

    a. Complete Sentence

    b. Fragment

Answers on page 147.

EXERCISE 3
Sentence Fragments

Directions: Decide if each sentence is a **fragment** or a **complete sentence**. **Write the correct answer in the space provided.**

1. While waiting for her neighbor to move the car that blocked the driveway.

2. Since Jean was not at the meeting, I took notes in her absence.

3. When my cousin moved to Dallas, Texas, after he graduated college.

4. My uncle has been running a charter school for five years.

5. So busy that he has little time for anything else.

6. To get to the stadium from your hotel, take a left out of the front entrance.

7. The largest source of revenue for the organization.

8. Larry deserves great praise and recognition.

9. Getting a great deal on a flight for your vacation.

10.   Research people who meditate.

Answers on page 147.

EXERCISE 4
Sentence Fragments

> **Directions:** Underline the **sentence fragment** in each paragraph. **Some paragraphs might contain more than one fragment.**

1. At the end of the business day, it is crucial for all employees to follow proper closing procedures for the breakroom. Before you leave. Make sure to wash all dirty dishes. And empty the trash of smelly food containers. The cleaning crew will trash everything left in the refrigerators at 5 p.m. every Friday.

2. Finding time for yourself. Is an important part of a healthy lifestyle. You may be neglecting your own physical and spiritual needs. If you are constantly focused on caring for other people. Research shows that people who set aside time to relax and enjoy life are actually better friends, co-workers and spouses. Than those who spend all their time accommodating others.

3. Getting a great deal on a flight for your next vacation is possible. If you can plan ahead and search several travel and airline websites. Buying 21 days in advance can save you a great deal of money. Also, try to fly after 7:00 p.m. Finally, shop around.

4. We are pleased to announce that Tireshia Davis is November's employee of the month. Meeting all company goals and a good team player. She will receive a $100 gift certificate to *Bed Bath & Beyond*. Please join us in congratulating Tireshia. When you see her around the office. Show your appreciation for her contributions to this department.

Answers on page 148.

Chapter 4

RUN-ON SENTENCES & COMMA SPLICES

What is a Run-on?

A run-on consists of two or more complete sentences joined together with no punctuation separating them. Run-on sentences are also called *fused* sentences.

> **Run-ons** are also called **fused** sentences. **Run-ons** and **fused** sentences are the same.

Example #1:

- This is a run on it goes on forever with no punctuation and jumps from subject to subject they are frustrating to read the brain wants order this is difficult to decipher the reader will stop paying attention and give up on your writing right about now

Example #2:

- Henry and Rose are both in their late **thirties** **they** decided to pay for their own wedding.

In the second example, the first complete sentence ends with the word *"thirties."* The second sentence begins with *"they."* Notice that no period ends the first sentence and no semicolon is used to properly connect these two short sentences.

In continuing to use the example of Henry and Rose, let's look at **four different ways** to correct run-on sentences.

1. MAKE TWO COMPLETE SENTENCES: USE A PERIOD

- **Correction #1:** Henry and Rose are both in their late **thirties. They** decided to pay for their own wedding.

2. USE A COMMA AND A COORDINATING CONJUNCTION

- **Correction #2:** Henry and Rose are both in their late **thirties, so they** decided to pay for their own wedding.

3. CONNECT SENTENCES: USE A SEMICOLON

- **Correction #3:** Henry and Rose are both in their late **thirties; they** decided to pay for their own wedding.

4. USE A SUBORDINATING CONJUNCTION

- **Correction #4:** **Since** Henry and Rose are both in their late **thirties, they** decided to pay for their own wedding.

> Comma splices are also called **comma faults.**

What is a Comma Splice?

A **comma splice** occurs when two complete sentences are separated by a comma instead of a period or a semicolon. In addition to being a grammar error, comma splices also create punctuation (mechanics) errors, since the wrong type of punctuation is used to separate sentences. Comma splices are also called **comma faults.**

✎ **Comma splices** are corrected in the same way as **run-on sentences**.

Example #1:

- Rhemona recently opened a photography studio, she also works as a dental hygienist.

1. MAKE TWO COMPLETE SENTENCES: USE A PERIOD

- **Correction #1:** Rhemona recently opened a photography studio. **She** also works as a dental hygienist.

2. USE A COMMA AND A COORDINATING CONJUNCTION

- **Correction #2:** Rhemona recently opened a photography studio**, and** she also works as a dental hygienist.

3. CONNECT SENTENCES: USE A SEMICOLON

- **Correction #3:** Rhemona recently opened a photography studio**;** she also works as a dental hygienist.

4. USE A SUBORDINATING CONJUNCTION

- **Correction #4:** Rhemona recently opened a photography studio, **although** she also works as a dental hygienist.

OR

- **Although** she also works as a dental hygienist, Rhemona recently opened a photography studio.

Knowledge Check

1. A _____ does not contain any punctuation.

2. Two complete sentences stuck together are _____.

3. Another name for a comma splice is a _____.

Answers at bottom of page.

1. run-on 2. fused 3. comma fault

EXERCISE 1
Run-on (Fused) Sentences

Directions: Identify each sentence as a **run-on** or a **complete sentence**. Write the correct answer in the space provided. **Insert correct punctuation marks where needed.**

1. The chocolate chips can be melted in the microwave the eggs can be added one at a time in the bowl.

2. David's cat cringed at the sight of the can of flea powder.

3. Deer roamed the wooded area long before developers built homes there.

4. Shop once a week stick to a preplanned grocery list.

5. Admitting to cheating on his girlfriend was honestly difficult for Marco.

6. Marnie loves scary movies Tony her boyfriend, refuses to watch them.

7. Dorothy Woods won the Business Woman of the Year award from the Junior League.

8. Your buttermilk biscuits taste superb they are the best I've ever eaten.

9. D'Andre applied for a small business loan to open a barbershop.

10. Margarine costs less than butter it contains less saturated fat.

Answers on page 148.

EXERCISE 2
Run-on (Fused) Sentences

Directions: Identify each sentence as a **run-on** or a **complete sentence**. Write the correct answer in the space provided. **Add punctuation and capitalization, if needed.**

1. The magazine sells for seventy-five cents in Canada it costs eighty cents.

2. Clouds of smoke filling the train cabins frightened the passengers.

3. The singer included several unannounced songs in the live show she changed the program.

4. They taught the parrot how to speak its words were indistinguishable.

5. Search carefully for grandma's old recipe book there are several places in the attic to look.

6. Using real butter is the key to baking great potato skins.

7. Concert pianists must practice six to eight hours a day.

8. Hot dogs are a typical American food Mrs. Roosevelt served them in the White House.

9. My cat sleeps on her special blanket every night.

10. A butterfly's wings are too large for efficient flying.

Answers on page 149.

EXERCISE 3
Comma Splices (Fault)

Directions: Circle the **correct answer** below.

1. Veronica's sister served as her doula, she wanted no one else at the birth.

    a. comma splice   b. correct

2. The mayor has a previous engagement, the meeting must be postponed.

    a. comma splice   b. correct

3. Joe Biden will not enter the 2016 presidential race.

    a. comma splice   b. correct

4. Mr. Myles claims he is sixty-eight, he is actually seventy-three.

    a. comma splice   b. correct

5. The conference rooms are small and lack amenities, but the hotel is lovely and the staff is courteous.

    a. comma splice   b. correct

6. Two diabetic parents tend to produce diabetic children.

    a. comma splice   b. correct

7. McClellan High School is low performing, the school board refuses to close it.

    a. comma splice   b. correct

8. Christmas decorations are available, Thanksgiving is still a month away.

    a. comma splice   b. correct

9. All radio broadcasting stocks have declined for the third consecutive day, yet trading remains brisk and optimistic.

    a. comma splice   b. correct

10. American history is being revised to ignore the human rights atrocities committed against minority groups.

    a. comma splice   b. correct

Answers on page 149.

EXERCISE 4
Run-ons & Comma Splices

Directions: Identify the following sentences as **comma splices** or **run-ons**. Write **correct** for sentences with no errors. **Make corrections as needed.**

1. Concussions are a huge problem in football too many players are suffering.

2. Tell your visitors not to park in front of the building, their cars will be towed.

3. My father does not watch football. He does not enjoy sports.

4. Dell's band will open for Boney James in Memphis and Little Rock, he will travel alone to the show in Dallas.

5. Marsha started a blog for natural health, but her writing is terrible.

6. People who take Zumba classes are much happier than those who cycle no research supports these statements, just my personal opinion.

7. Tiffany applied for an executive assistant position, the interviewer said her name sounded too young for the seasoned staff on the job.

8. Nathan changed his status to "in a relationship" on Facebook he received many likes.

9. Evelyn over sang her original song at the gospel festival, so the DJ cut the music early she continued to sing a capella, until the host took the stage.

10. Friends come, friends go. Such is life.

Answers on page 149.

Chapter 5

PREPOSITIONS

What is a Preposition?

- Prepositions are function words that show relationship between subjects, objects and other parts of a sentence.

- Prepositions also describe location or position by showing where or in relation to what (*e.g.* above, behind).

- In addition to spatial relationships, prepositions also clarify time or temporal relationships (*e.g.* before, after).

- A preposition must have an object (noun or pronoun) following it. This is called the **object of the preposition**.

- The combination of the preposition and its object is called a **prepositional phrase**.

Examples:

- The dance studio sits **behind the Walgreens on Main Street**.

- Sylvia left her purse **in the restaurant**.

- Go **into the house** right now.

- Donnie left **without saying goodbye**.

Ending Sentences with Prepositions

1. Contrary to popular belief and long-standing American language customs, **you can end a sentence with a preposition**. This should not be counted as a grammatical error, but rather a questionable choice of writing style.

2. Although you want to avoid doing so in formal essays or reports, it is acceptable for the casual speaker or the casual writer to end a statement or question with a preposition.

3. If attempting to avoid ending sentences with a preposition sounds awkward or strange, just use the preposition or reword the sentence altogether.

4. Again, putting prepositions at the end of sentences is not a grammatical error. It is a matter of personal preference and writing style.

5. In formal writing, social or educational settings, **it is best to avoid ending sentences with prepositions.**

> ## In **casual writing** or informal conversations, you can **end sentences** with **prepositions**.

Examples:

- Where did all this money come **from**?

- Where did you get all this money?

- Where did Stack say to meet him **at**?

- Where did Stack tell us to meet him?

- What state did Melanie move **to**?

- Where did Melanie move? What state?

- To what state did Melanie move?   (**Too awkward!**)

As you can see from the examples above, it is **possible** and **preferable** to **avoid ending** sentences with **prepositions**.

Knowledge Check

1. A _____ shows relationship between nouns and objects.

2. The _____ is a noun that follows the preposition.

3. A _____ includes a preposition and its object.

Answers at bottom of page.

Types of Prepositions

- Common Prepositions
- Compound Prepositions
- Phrasal Prepositions

How do you recognize a preposition? What words or phrases count as prepositions? In order to identify prepositions in real-world writing, you must begin to memorize them, until they become familiar to you. To get started, **review the lists of prepositions** on the following pages.

How do you identify these different types of prepositions?

➤ **Common prepositions** are usually just one word.

➤ **Compound prepositions** consist of two words.

➤ **Phrasal prepositions** contain three or more words.

1. preposition 2. object of the preposition 3. prepositional phrase

Common Prepositions

aboard	down
about	during
above	except
across	following
after	for
against	from
along	in
alongside	inside
amid	into
among	like
around	near
as	of
at	off
because	on
before	onto
behind	opposite
below	outside
beneath	over
beside	past
besides	regarding
between	round
beyond	since
by	
considering	
concerning	
despite	

More Common Prepositions

than	unto
through	up
throughout	upon
to	versus
toward	via
under	with
underneath	within
unlike	without
until	

Compound & Phrasal Prepositions

according to	because of
ahead of	by means of
all over	by way of
apart from	close by
as early as	close to
as for	contrary to
as late as	due to
as many as	except for
as much	in addition to
as of	in back of
as often as	in between
aside from	in case of
in comparison with	in contrast to

in front of

in keeping with

in lieu of

in place of

in spite of

instead of

in view of

near to

next to

on behalf of

on top of

other than

out of

owing to

similar to

together with

up to

with regard to

with respect to

EXERCISE 1
Prepositions

Directions: Cross out all **prepositional phrases** in the sentences below.

1. Roslyn became a successful corporate accountant in spite of her traumatic childhood.

2. Perry always meditates before writing a sermon.

3. Braylon hid his favorite cookies behind the microwave.

4. One of Carla's extensions fell out of her hair during our cardio kick boxing class.

5. A generous client sent Stephen an expensive bottle of wine for landing a huge contract.

6. Nina should have checked the weather reports before washing her car.

7. Many bank tellers cannot tell the difference between a fake $100 bill and a real one.

8. Alice Walker is best known for her novel *The Color Purple*.

9. Your first direct deposit should post by the last Friday of this month.

10. Since her car stopped running a few days ago, Rhonda has not left the house.

Answers on page 150.

EXERCISE 2
Prepositions

Directions: **First**, cross out any **prepositional phrases** in these sentences. **Next circle the subjects and underline the verbs.**

1. Jamarion bought the jogging suit with blue pinstripes.

2. I missed my bus more often than not last month.

3. The new computer course was filled with students by the first hour of registration.

4. The job was a good opportunity for Orlando to learn about merchandising.

5. The Arkansas Razorbacks were thrilled with their triple overtime victory.

6. Two of my neighbors have been feuding over parking spaces for weeks.

7. In the course of three days, forest fires destroyed most of the national park.

8. Two-paycheck families are becoming less common in this crazy economy.

9. For a skilled tailor, sewing a skirt presents no problem.

10. The Million Man March changed the lives of millions of people.

Answers on page 150.

EXERCISE 3
Prepositions

Directions: Circle the correct **preposition** for each sentence.

1. I will take the GRE _____ January 2020.

    a. in
    b. on

2. _____ June of 1863, the Confederate forces pushed north to Pennsylvania.

    a. In
    b. On

3. According _____ a recent study, daily servings of broccoli reduce incidences of high blood pressure.

    a. to
    b. from

4. You will find the encyclopedias _____ the reference room.

    a. on
    b. in

5. Many philosophers are opposed _____ capital punishment.

    a. to
    b. about

6. My apartment building is _____ the corner of First Avenue and 14th Street.

    a. on
    b. in

7. I'll take responsibility _____ all administrative errors.
    a. for
    b . from

8. _____ Mondays, Wednesdays and Fridays, Philip goes to the gym.

    a. In
    b. On

9. Heidi's addicted _____ caffeine; she can't start the day without a cup of coffee.

     a. with

     b. to

10. Mona studied _____ the library until it closed.

     a. on

     b. in

Answers on page 151.

Chapter 6

SUBJECT-VERB AGREEMENT

What is Subject-Verb Agreement?

Maintaining subject-verb agreement in sentences means that the number of the subject matches the number of the verb. Basically, a singular subject agrees with a singular verb. The same is true for plural subjects and plural verbs.

For example: <u>**Eileen**</u> <u>**walks**</u> three miles per day.

In this sentence, **Eileen** is the **subject**. Eileen is only one person. The verb that describes her actions must also be singular. Singular subject; singular verb.

- <u>**Eileen**</u> = singular subject

- <u>**walks**</u> = singular verb

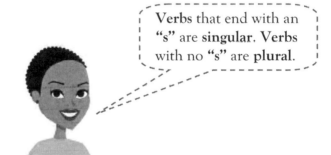

Verbs that end with an "s" are **singular**. **Verbs** with no "s" are **plural**.

- Remember, verbs that end in **"s"** are considered singular verbs. Verbs with no **"s"** at the end are plural verbs. **Please note:** this rule does not apply to irregular verbs.

Rules of Subject-Verb Agreement

1. The subject and the verb must agree in number.
2. Singular subjects take singular verbs.
3. Plural subjects take plural verbs.

Examples:

> ➤ A price <u>list</u> <u>hangs</u> on the front counter.

> <u>list</u>   = singular subject

> <u>hangs</u> = singular verb

> ➤ Their <u>dogs</u> <u>bark</u> constantly.

> <u>dogs</u> = plural subject

> <u>bark</u> = plural verb

Subject-Verb Agreement: Clauses

> The **subject** and **verb** must **agree** in **number** even when separated by phrases and clauses.

Example:

- <u>Money</u>, as well as staff and equipment, <u>is needed</u> for the project.

In this example, the **subject**, <u>money</u>, is separated from the verb by a prepositional phrase. The **verb** consists of two words – <u>is needed</u>.

money   = singular subject

is needed = singular verb (helping + main verb)

Remember, in order to find the subject, cross out the prepositional phrases.

- <u>Money</u>, ~~as well as staff and equipment~~, <u>is needed</u> ~~for the project~~.

Once you cross out the prepositional phrases, the subject and the verb are clear and apparent, which makes subject–verb agreement easier to maintain.

Notice that even without the prepositional phrases, the sentence still makes sense, but lacks the description and clarity that prepositional phrases provide.

Subject-Verb Agreement: Compound Subjects

> Compound subjects joined by **"and"** require plural verbs.

- **Example #1:**

    Peanut butter and jelly mix well together.

    - **peanut butter and jelly** = plural subject
    - **mix** = plural verb

- **Example #2:**

    Jay-Z and Beyoncé earn millions of dollars each year.

    - Jay-Z and Beyoncé = plural subject
    - earn = plural verb

Subject-Verb Agreement: Singular /Compound Subjects

> A compound subject joined by **"or"** or **"nor"** takes a singular verb.

- **Example #1:**

    The chairman or the president is willing to discuss the financial goals for the year.

    - chairman or the president = compound subject
    - or = singular conjunction
    - is willing = singular verb

In this example, the subject consists of two people: the **chairman** and the **president**. Two or more means compound. Since chairman and president are singular and joined by the conjunction **"or,"** these two nouns form a **compound subject** that needs a singular verb, because the conjunction **"or"** takes a singular verb. However, the exception to this rule is illustrated in example three on the next page.

- **Example #2:**

  The <u>instructor nor the dean</u> <u>knows</u> how to address the student.

  - <u>instructor nor the dean</u> = compound subject
  - <u>nor</u> = singular conjunction
  - <u>knows</u> = singular verb

> **SPECIAL NOTE:** If one of the nouns in the compound subject is **singular** and the other is **plural**, use the noun **closest** to the verb to establish subject-verb agreement.

- **Example #3:**

  The homeroom <u>teacher</u> or the <u>aides</u> <u>serve</u> breakfast in the mornings.

  - <u>aides</u> = plural noun (**subject**) closest to the verb
  - <u>serve</u> = plural verb

Subject-Verb Agreement: Either or/ Neither Nor

> In **either/or** and **neither/nor** constructions, the verb agrees with the nearest subject.

- **Example #1:**

  Either the <u>employer</u> or the <u>employees</u> <u>arrange</u> monthly lunch outings.

In this example, the **compound subject** — <u>employer or employees</u> — is joined by the **either/or** paired conjunction. The second subject (employees) — the one after the **"or"** — determines if the verb will be singular or plural.

In this case, **"employees"** is positioned closest to the verb, <u>arrange</u>. The subject **"employees"** is plural. Therefore, the verb must be plural in order to achieve subject-verb agreement.

  - <u>employer or employees</u> = compound subject
  - <u>employees</u> = plural subject closest to the verb
  - <u>arrange</u> = plural verb

- **Example #2:**

  Neither the <u>buyers</u> **nor** the <u>sales manager</u> <u>favors</u> the price increase.

  - <u>buyers nor the sales manager</u> = compound subject
  - <u>sales manager</u> = singular subject closest to the verb
  - <u>favors</u> = singular verb

Subject-Verb Agreement: Indefinite Pronouns (Singular)

> ## Use a **singular verb** after these **indefinite pronoun** subjects.

- Another
- Anybody
- Anyone
- Each
- Each one
- Either
- Every
- Everybody

- Everyone
- Much
- Neither
- No one
- Nobody
- One
- Somebody
- Someone

- **Example #1:**

  <u>Each</u> of the reports <u>needs</u> to be stapled and filed.

- **Example #2:**

  <u>Nobody</u> <u>wants</u> to be alone during the holidays.

- **Example #3:**

  <u>Everybody</u> <u>works</u> for the weekend.

- **Example #4:**

  To whom <u>much</u> <u>is</u> given, <u>much</u> <u>is</u> required.

Subject-Verb Agreement: Indefinite Pronouns (Plural)

> Use a **plural verb** after these **indefinite pronoun** subjects.

- Both
- Few
- Many

- Other (s)
- Several

Examples:

- Both <u>supervise</u> the group.

- Many <u>were invited</u>, but few <u>were able</u> to attend.

Subject-Verb Agreement: Collective Nouns

> If the **group** is acting as a **unit**, use a **singular verb**.

- **Example #1:**

  - The **Board of Directors** <u>meets</u> on Wednesday.

- **Example #2:**

  - The **staff** <u>supports</u> the move.

In the above examples, **Board of Directors** and **staff** are referred to as single units, despite the appearance of being plural. Singular subjects take singular verbs. Therefore, the verbs **"meets"** and **"supports"** must end with an **"s"** to form the singular.

Remember:

> Singular subjects take singular verbs. Plural subjects take plural verbs.

If the members of the **group** are **acting separately**, use a **plural verb**.

Example #1:

- The <u>council</u> <u>are divided</u> about the school bond issue.

Explanation: If the council is divided about an issue, then the group is not acting as a unit. Some members believe one way and the rest believe another way. Since there is no unanimous agreement, the council is acting as two separate groups. Therefore, the verb — <u>are divided</u> — is plural.

Example #2:

- The <u>majority</u> <u>refuse</u> to contribute to the office party.

Explanation: The subject, <u>majority,</u> suggests that most of the group refuses to contribute to the office party, but not everyone participates in this action. Since the group is not acting in agreement as a single unit, the verb — <u>refuse</u> — is plural.

Example #3:

- The <u>jury</u> <u>disagree</u> on the defendant's innocence.

Explanation: Because the jury disagrees on a decision, this group is acting as separate voting members. Therefore, the verb — <u>disagree</u> — is plural.

Example #4:

- The <u>volunteer committee</u> <u>split</u> their duties by morning and evening shifts.

Explanation: Since part of the volunteers work in the morning and others in the evening, the committee is not acting as one single unit, but as separate groups. Therefore, the verb — <u>split</u> — is plural.

EXERCISE 1
Subject-Verb Agreement

Directions: A blank space appears where a verb should be. Decide which verb agrees with the subject of the sentence. **Circle the letter that indicates your choice.**

1. Connecticut _____ two nicknames: the Constitution State and the Nutmeg State.

   a. has

   b. have

2. Whenever my family _____ to a baseball game, we all _____ hot dogs and pretzels.

   a. go, gets

   b. goes, get

3. One of the car's six cylinders _____ not working.

   a. are

   b. is

4. The candidate's record on health-care reform is what _____ Margaret.

   a. impress

   b. impresses

5. Here _____ my check for the first month's rent and the security deposit.

   a. is

   b. are

6. One of the dentists _____ close to the office.

   a. live

   b. lives

7. My cat often _____ the mail carrier.

   a. chase

   b. chases

8. Each of those pastry desserts _____ salty and undercooked.

        a. taste

        b. tastes

9. Neither the buyer nor the seller_____ with the lawyer's suggestion for the closing date on the house.

        a. agree

        b. agrees

10. Where is the driver who usually _____ this route?

        a. runs

        b. run

Answers on page 151.

EXERCISE 2
Subject-Verb Agreement

Directions: Circle the word that correctly completes each sentence.

1. Meat from sheep more than eighteen months old **(is, are)** mutton.

2. Gas ranges with electric ignitions **(use, uses)** less gas than those with pilot lights.

3. Cargo ships that do not have fixed routes **(is, are)** known as tramps.

4. Ambrosia, the food of the gods according to Greek mythology, **(give, gives)** those who eat it eternal youth and beauty.

5. Narrow fingers of land extending into a body of water **(is, are)** called spits.

6. Ray, along with two of his friends, **(plans, plan)** to visit Miami.

7. The planes on the runway **(follows, follow)** the taxiway to the terminal.

8. The leaves of the cherry tree **(is, are)** poisonous.

9. Photographs taken from space **(pinpoints, pinpoint)** exact locations on the earth's surface.

10. The crooked alternator draining Arturos' new battery **(frustrate, frustrates)** his plans for a weekend getaway road trip.

Answers on page 151.

EXERCISE 3
Subject-Verb Agreement

Directions: Circle the word that correctly completes each sentence.

1. Neither Jana nor David **(want, wants)** to work in retail forever.

2. Both the subway and the bus **(stop, stops)** near the post office.

3. Either John or his coworkers **(check, checks)** the mail each day.

4. Locks or an alarm **(provide, provides)** some security against burglaries.

5. Both the carrots and the sweet potato **(furnish, furnishes)** vitamin A to the body.

6. Neither Colorado nor the mountain states **(is, are)** known for mild winters.

7. Both New York and Texas **(offer, offers)** great educational opportunities.

8. Poor spelling and grammar **(interferes, interfere)** with effective communication.

9. Each person in my office **(look, looks)** tired.

10. Every morning, Janet **(jog, jogs)** to work.

Answers on page 151.

EXERCISE 4
Subject-Verb Agreement

Directions: Circle the word that correctly completes each sentence below.

1. Either coffee or tea **(is, are)** served during the refreshment breaks.

2. The greatest nuisance **(is, are)** the refunds we have to process.

3. Each of the supervisors **(needs, need)** a planning calendar.

4. The committee **(has, have)** agreed to submit the report next week.

5. Neither the president nor the membership **(was, were)** in favor of meeting weekly.

6. This study, as well as many earlier studies, **(shows, show)** that turnover is declining steadily.

7. A system of lines **(extends, extend)** horizontally to form a grid.

8. Either May or June **(is, are)** a good time for the regional conference.

9. The panel, consisting of outstanding representatives from private industry and government, **(has agreed, have agreed)** to accept questions on the report.

10. Everybody in the meeting **(was, were)** becoming restless as discussions continued.

Answers on page 151.

Chapter 7

NOUN-PRONOUN AGREEMENT

What is Noun-Pronoun Agreement?

A noun (antecedent) and its pronoun must agree in person, number and gender. Basically, a noun and pronoun must both be written in first, second or third person. Singular nouns take singular pronouns. Plural nouns take plural pronouns. Female nouns take female pronouns and masculine nouns require masculine pronouns in order to achieve proper noun–pronoun agreement.

Definitions to Know

Person: Refers to the subject or the person who is speaking.
First person pronouns: "I" or "we."
Second person: "you."
Third person: "he, she, it, they."

What is **person**?

Number: Refers to whether the subject and pronouns are **singular** or **plural**; one or more than one.

What is **number**?

Gender: Refers to whether the nouns and pronouns are masculine or feminine; **male** or **female**.

What is **gender**?

Examples:

- *Shannon* wants to know whether *her* proposal has been accepted.

- The grand *jury* has completed *its* investigation.

- *I* must support *my* client, as *you* must support *yours*.

91

Types of Pronouns

Nominative (Subject) Pronouns:
Function as subjects; "naming" pronouns.

I, he, she, we, who, you, they, it

Objective (Object) Pronouns:
Function as objects of verbs or objects of prepositions.

me, him, her, us, them, whom, you, it

Possessive Pronouns:
Show ownership; no apostrophes are needed to show possession.

my/mine, his, her/hers, our/ours, their/theirs, whose, your/yours, its

PRONOUN CHART

Nominative (Subjects)	I	he	she	we	they	who	you	it
Objective (Objects)	me	him	her	us	them	whom	you	it
Possessive (Ownership)	my mine	his	her hers	our ours	their theirs	whose	your yours	its

Noun-Pronoun Agreement: Singular

Singular nouns must be matched with **singular pronouns** to achieve agreement within the sentence.

Examples:

- *Gregory* researched ***his*** New Orleans family roots.

- *You* must pay ***your*** own tuition fees.

- *Ashua* released ***her*** barriers to love and got engaged.

 **Remember,** the **antecedent** is the word or noun that the pronoun refers to or replaces. The antecedent usually comes **before** the pronoun. The **pronoun** usually follows or comes **after** the antecedent. Pronouns reduce repetition when referring back to the antecedent.

Example:

- Jana took <u>the book</u> from the shelf and gave <u>the book</u> to Chris.

- Jana took <u>the book</u> from the shelf and gave <u>it</u> to Chris.

the book	=	antecedent
it	=	pronoun (object)

Singular Subject Pronouns	Singular Object Pronouns	Singular Possessive Pronouns
I	me	my, mine
you	you	your, yours
he, she, it	him, her, it	his, her, hers, its

Noun-Pronoun Agreement: Plural

Plural nouns must be matched with **plural pronouns** to achieve agreement within the sentence.

Examples:

- <u>Deborah and Jean</u> left ***their*** bibles at church.

- <u>Rickey</u> baked cakes and sold ***them*** to local diners.

- The <u>football players</u> lost, but ***they*** ate pizza after the game.

Plural Subject Pronouns	Plural Object Pronouns	Plural Possessive Pronouns
we	us	our, ours
you	you	your, yours
they	them	their, theirs

Special Cases: Correlative Conjunctions

When nouns and pronouns are joined by the correlative conjunctions — **either/or,** **neither/ nor, but/also, not/only** — use the second noun or the one **closest to the verb** to choose a singular or plural pronoun.

Examples:

- **Either** Dan **or** Terry **(singular noun)** will have to give up <u>his</u> **(singular pronoun)** office.

- **Neither** Tara **nor** her **daughters (plural noun)** asked <u>their</u> **(plural pronoun)** husbands for money.

- **Not only** the executive assistants, **but also** the **manager (singular noun)** needs to turn in <u>her</u> **(singular pronoun)** timecard by Friday afternoon.

Indefinite Pronouns: Singular

Some **pronouns** are always **singular.** Always treat the following indefinite pronouns as singular in noun-pronoun and subject-verb agreement. **Remember, you cannot determine correct grammar by the way you speak or the way words sound when you say them aloud.** So, avoid the temptation to make these particular pronouns plural.

Always consider these **indefinite pronouns** as **singular:**

all	every	no one
any	everybody	nothing
anybody	everyone	one
anyone	everything	other
anything	neither	some
each	nobody	someone
either	none	something

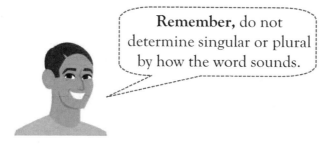

Example #1:

- <u>Every</u> cat in the neighborhood scratches *its* back on Mr. and Mrs. Humphrey's oak tree.

• **every**	=	singular indefinite pronoun
• **its**	=	singular possessive pronoun

Example #2:

- <u>Each</u> of the participants has given *his or her* approval to be photographed at the event.

• **each**	=	singular indefinite pronoun
• **his or her**	=	singular possessive pronoun

Special Note:

His or her constructions are grammatically correct but stylistically awkward. Try to make subjects and pronouns plural to **avoid writing his/her.**

Example #3:

- <u>One</u> of the maintenance men lost *his* wallet in the parking lot.

  o **one** = singular indefinite pronoun
  o **his** = singular possessive pronoun

<u>Indefinite Pronouns: Plural</u>

Some **pronouns** are always **plural**. Always treat the following indefinite pronouns as plural in noun-pronoun and subject-verb agreement.

both	few	many	several	others

Examples:

- The <u>few</u> who have completed *their* research assignments may leave class early.

- The teacher asked <u>both</u> of the students if *they* cheated on the math test.

- <u>Several</u> dental patients confess that *they* only brush once a day.

Indefinite Pronouns: Both Plural and Singular

Some pronouns function as **both plural and singular**, depending on how they are used in a sentence.

all	most	some	any	none	more

Examples:

- <u>All</u> of the tenants paid *their* rent money on time.

In this example, the indefinite pronoun <u>all</u> refers to *tenants*, which is a plural noun. Although the plural noun "*tenants*" is located within a prepositional phrase and cannot be the subject, it still determines whether or not <u>all</u> is singular or plural. In this case, <u>all</u> is plural.

- <u>All</u> of the sugar is still in *its* container.

In this example, the indefinite pronoun <u>all</u> refers to *sugar*, which is a **singular** noun. Therefore, in this case, <u>all</u> is singular.

Rule of Thumb

If the indefinite pronoun refers to something that can be counted (**tenants**), make it **plural**. If the object cannot be counted (**sugar**), make it **singular**.

Examples:

- <u>Some</u> of the girls rented *their* prom dresses instead of buying new ones.

In this example, the indefinite pronoun <u>some</u> refers to *girls*, which is a plural noun. In this case, <u>some</u> is plural.

- <u>**Some**</u> of the footwear in this store is not worth *its* price.

In this example, the indefinite pronoun <u>some</u> refers to *footwear*, which is a singular noun. In this case, <u>some</u> is singular.

Collective Nouns

Examples of Collective Nouns

army, audience, board, cabinet, class, committee, company, corporation, council department, faculty, family, firm, group, jury, majority, minority, public, school, team

When **collective nouns** refer to a group that is acting as a **single unit** — everybody agrees and acts as one body — the **collective** or group **noun** is **singular** and requires a **singular pronoun**.

Examples:

- The <u>**committee**</u> submitted *its* annual budget to the Dean.

- The Connor <u>**family**</u> changed *its* final answer on *Family Feud*.

When **collective nouns** refer to a group that is acting as **individual members** — members disagree or take separate actions — the **collective** or group **noun** is **plural** and requires a **plural pronoun**.

Examples:

- The <u>**faculty**</u> disagreed on how to get *their* salaries raised.

- The <u>**audience**</u> returned to *their* seats after intermission.

Specific Organizations

Unlike collective nouns, **specific organizations** — schools, small businesses, corporations, churches — are always considered singular and require **singular pronouns**.

Examples:

- **Parkview High School** supported *its* band by selling candy.
- **Mama B's** restaurant posted *its* menu on the order window.

Relative Pronouns: Who/ Whoever

- Use **who** or **whoever** if you can substitute the following pronouns for the "who":

  - he
  - she
  - they
  - I
  - we

> **Who** or **whoever** refers to **subjects** of sentences.

Examples:

- **Who** is waiting?
  - **He/She** is waiting.
- **Who** did they say was chosen?
  - **He/ She/ I** was chosen.
- The job goes to **whoever** answers the ad first.
  - **He/She** answered the ad first.

Relative Pronouns: Whom/ Whomever

As with **who** and **whoever**, the relative pronouns **whom** and **whomever** cause quite a bit of confusion for some people. Many people botch the usage of these particular pronouns in efforts to 'sound' smart. However, the rules for engagement, so to speak, are quite simple to remember.

- Use **whom** or **whomever** if you can substitute the following pronouns:

  - him
  - her
  - them
  - me
  - us

Remember, **whom/whomever** (and the related pronouns above), **function** as **objects of verbs** or **objects of prepositions.**

Examples:

- **Whom** did you ask to pick up the order?

  - I asked **him/ her/ them** to pick up the order.

- Mary is polite to **whomever** she speaks to regardless of the situation.

  - Mary is polite to **him/ her/ them/ me/ us.**

> **Reminders**
>
> 1. Who/whoever refers to **subjects.**
>
> 2. Whom/whomever refers to **objects of verbs** or **objects of prepositions.**

Knowledge Check

1. Sharon will complain to _____ answers the phone.

2. With _____ did you verify the budget before buying iPads?

3. _____ did you say was chosen for the teaching position?

Answers at bottom of page.

1. Whomever 2. Whom 3. Who

EXERCISE 1
Noun-Pronoun Agreement

Directions: Choose the correct **pronouns** to fill in the blanks.

1. Louis and _____ majored in economics because _____ are fascinated with world finance.

        a. me, I   c. I, we

        b. me, we

2. Neither Jack nor Bill remembered to bring _____ membership card to the gym.

        a. his   c. they're

        b. their

3. One of the hotel guests left _____ purse on the couch in the lobby.

        a. she   c. his or her

        b. their

4. The University Judiciary Board, composed of twelve undergraduate students, reached _____ decision on the date rape case.

        a. their   c. his or her

        b. its

5. At the concert hall, _____ said that I could leave Donna's ticket at the box office.

        a. him and her   c. they

        b. them

6. Jonathan and _____ thought that skydiving might be fun to try.

        a. I   c. her

        b. me

7. Everyone must bring _____ own chair to the outdoor jazz concert.

        a. their   c. his or her

        b. our

8. The cab driver told Vic and _____ that traffic on the bridge was heavy at this time of day.

        a. me   c. myself

        b. I

9. The company launched _____ new environmental campaign today.

        a. their   c. it's

        b. its

10. _____ has never been to Disneyland or Epcot will go with _____ this July.

        a. Whomever, us   c. Whoever, us

        b. Whoever, we

Answers on page 152.

EXERCISE 2
Noun-Pronoun Agreement

Directions: Read each sentence carefully. **Circle the correct response.**

1. On Mother's Day, Maura rented *The Color Purple* because it is (**she, her**) mother's favorite movie.

2. The committee nominated Sandra Jimenez, (**their, its**) favorite candidate.

3. Every woman on the basketball team brought (**her, their**) date to the banquet.

4. Neither of the two fathers could find (**their, his**) son in the enormous museum.

5. (**He/Everybody**) said that Laina can leave early for her doctor's appointment.

6. (**It, The voicemail greeting**) states that the store is open from 9 to 5.

7. (**She, Her**) and I have been close friends since college.

8. I hope you have more fun camping than (**me, I**).

9. To (**whom, who**) shall I direct your call?

10. My brother and (**I, myself**) arrived at Gina's party on time.

Answers on page 152.

EXERCISE 3
Noun-Pronoun Agreement

Directions: Read each sentence carefully. **Circle the correct pronoun**.

1. A few of the researchers felt that **(he or she, they)** had discovered a safe alternative to Viagra.

2. Neither of the managers planned to change **(his or her, their)** work team.

3. Most of the instructors expect bonuses in **(his or her, their)** paychecks.

4. Some of the Christmas toy donations will find **(its, their)** way into the pockets of unscrupulous community volunteers.

5. None of the organic farmers felt that an increase in consumer interest would overwhelm **(his or her, their)** resources.

6. Few of today's teenagers are loyal to one brand of clothing even though **(he or she, they)** may prefer one over another.

7. Only one of the parents at the PTA meeting expected to pay for **(her, their)** child's school t-shirt.

8. Anyone can make a good first impression on **(his or her, their)** job interview.

9. Many law firms have asked **(its, their)** executives to recruit at local colleges.

10. Every woman loves a man until **(her, their)** trust is broken.

Answers on page 152.

Chapter 8

DANGLING & MISPLACED MODIFIERS

What is a Modifier?

A **modifier** is a word or phrase that **describes** something. The modifier must be positioned close to whatever it is describing to avoid confusion.

What is a Dangling Modifier?

When a modifier is not properly attached to a subject, or whatever it is describing within the sentence, it is called a **dangling modifier.** Dangling modifiers are also called **dangling participles,** because they usually begin with an *-ing* gerund. However, not all dangling modifier phrases begin with an *-ing* word. An error occurs when the modifier phrase is separated from the noun it describes in a way that makes the sentence confusing. A dangling modifier is corrected by moving the phrase close to the noun (person, place or thing) it is describing. Secondly, the subject or the performer of the action, must be clear.

Example #1: Dangling Modifier

- Coming around the bend in the road, the church was seen.

Dangling modifiers can be tricky to detect, because readers often supply meaning that is not apparent in the sentence the way it is actually written.

Was the **church** seen coming around the bend?

Did **a person** come around the bend and see the church?

You might be tempted to assume that a person came around the bend and saw a church. However, the above example **lacks a subject** or an actual person to perform the action.

Correction:

- **Coming around the bend in the road,** <u>Cara</u> saw the church.

Now, it is clear that Cara, a person, performed the action in the sentence: **came** around the **bend** and **saw** the **church.**

However, another question arises that can be answered with further revision.

Did Cara **walk or drive** around the bend?

Revision:

- **While driving around the bend in the road**, <u>Cara</u> saw the small, country church not far from her grandparents' farm.

You have now learned to **correct dangling modifiers** and to **add descriptive details** for sentence variety and increased clarity.

Example #2: Dangling Modifier

- While working on the manuscript, the computer continually lapsed to sleep mode.

Did the **computer** keep falling asleep while working on the manuscript?
What **person** worked on the manuscript?

Corrections:

- While <u>Susan</u> <u>worked</u> on the manuscript, the computer continually lapsed to sleep mode.
- The computer continually lapsed to sleep mode while <u>Susan</u> <u>worked</u> on the manuscript.

The above example requires the addition of a **person**, <u>Susan</u>, and tweaks to the verb <u>work</u> from progressive (<u>working</u>) to simple past tense (<u>worked</u>) to fully clarify the action and its performer.

Example #3: Dangling Modifier

- Having read the instructions carefully, the bookcase was easily assembled.

Who read the instructions carefully?
Who assembled the bookcase?

Correction:

- Having read the instructions carefully, <u>**Derrick**</u> easily assembled the bookcase.

Example #4: Dangling Modifier

- The procedures manual was a welcome sight to Arthur lying on the desk.

Was **Arthur** lying on the desk or **the manual**?

Corrections:

- The procedures manual <u>lying on the desk</u> was a welcome sight to Arthur.
- <u>Lying on the desk</u>, the procedures manual was a welcome sight to Arthur.

What is a Misplaced Modifier?

When the modifier is not close to the word or phrase it describes, the resulting sentence can be ambiguous or even humorous.

The **incorrectly positioned** modifier is **misplaced**.

Example #1: Misplaced Modifier

- The manager issued a laptop to the assistant with removable storage.

Did the assistant have removable storage?

The phrase *with removable storage* is positioned right next to the word **"assistant,"** so the phrase actually describes or modifies the assistant. This phrase is considered misplaced, because the laptop logically contains removable storage, not the person, the assistant. Notice that the misplaced modifier is technically a prepositional phrase.

Move the misplaced modifier next to the word **"laptop"** to clarify the intended meaning of the sentence.

Correction:

- The manager issued a **laptop** <u>with removable storage</u> to the assistant.

Example #2: Misplaced Modifier

- Only the director paid for the terminal, not the software program.

Correction:

- The director <u>only</u> paid for the terminal, not the software program.

Example #3: Misplaced Modifier

- Patrick nearly won $1,000 on a scratch-off ticket.

How can you almost win the lottery?

Correction:

- Patrick won nearly $1,000 on a scratch-off ticket.

- Although you either win or lose a lottery by one number or several, it is possible to win nearly or approximately $1,000, such as $999.

Knowledge Check

1. A _____ occurs when a participle phrase is not attached to a subject.

2. A _____ is a descriptive phrase that is incorrectly placed.

3. A _____ is a word or phrase that describes something.

Answers at bottom of page.

1. dangling modifier 2. misplaced modifier 3. modifier

EXERCISE 1
Dangling & Misplaced Modifiers

Directions: Indicate whether the sentences below are **correct** or contain a **dangling modifier**. Use the letter **"C"** for **correct** and **"DM"** for **dangling modifier**.

_____ 1. Containing tennis courts and pools, some hotels are more like resorts.

_____ 2. Having watched the movie closely, the ending was confusing.

_____ 3. Viewing alcohol as a beverage, it is often not considered a drug.

_____ 4. Before the meeting began, Matt and Thomas photocopied the agenda and placed one in each chair.

_____ 5. Judging subliminal messages to be ineffective, such advertisements were abandoned in the 1950s.

_____ 6. Trying to decide whether to buy a mask of Kim Kardashian or of Frankenstein, Joey lingered thoughtfully by the drugstore display.

_____ 7. Imagining that life exists on Titan, one of Saturn's moons, many science fiction stories have been written.

_____ 8. Signifying that too many Americans have forgotten what Memorial Day means, the parade attracted a very small crowd.

_____ 9. Having been laid off from his job in an aircraft factory, Virgil became a detective in order to pay his mortgage.

_____ 10. Riding on a rubber raft, Leslie and Colleen traveled down the Snake River.

Answers on page 152.

EXERCISE 2
Dangling & Misplaced Modifiers

Directions: Rewrite each sentence to correct the dangling or misplaced modifier. Use commas and add words when necessary.

1. Plump sausages, the dinner guests looked forward to the main course.

2. Soaring over the treetops in a hot air balloon, the view was spectacular.

3. Powered by hydrogen, the engineers designed a new kind of car.

4. I introduced my boyfriend to my father, who wanted to marry me.

5. Revised to highlight his computer expertise, Marcelo was proud of his new resumé.

6. Jim, who loved to lick car windows, drove his dog to the vet.

7. Banging inside the dryer, Carla heard the lost keys.

8. We complained about the proposed building to the mayor, which we found ugly and too large for the neighborhood.

9. Covered with whipped cream, Brandon carried a chocolate cake.

10. A homeless teenager, the nun helped the girl find a place to live.

Answers on page 152-153.

EXERCISE 3
Dangling & Misplaced Modifiers

Directions: Rewrite each sentence to **correct** the **dangling** or **misplaced modifier**. Use **commas** and add words when necessary.

1. Slowly cooling off, I took a sip of tea.

2. Departing on track 12, the commuter anxiously rushed ahead.

3. The weather got worse driving down the interstate.

4. Having received your check, a new bill will be sent out.

5. Crying inconsolably, the tears kept flowing long after the movie ended.

Answers on page 154-155.

Chapter 9

HOMONYMS & HOMOPHONES

What is a Homonym?

Homonyms are words that share the same spelling and same (or similar) pronunciation, but different meanings. Homonyms are also called **look-a-likes**.

- **Same** spelling
- **Same** pronunciation
- **Different** meanings

Examples:

- <u>Scale</u> the fish.

    Verb: to scale

- Weigh the fish on the <u>scale</u>.

    Noun: a scale

Homonyms are also called **look-a-likes**.

Examples of Homonyms

1. **tire:** a wheel on a vehicle   **tire:** to get fatigued
2. **bear:** large animal   **bear:** to support
3. **band:** a group   **band:** to unite
4. **tip:** pointed or slender end   **tip:** giving money
5. **suit:** set of clothing   **suit:** to satisfy
6. **sole:** bottom of a shoe   **sole:** the only one

What is a Homophone?

Homophones are words that share the same pronunciation, different spellings and different meanings. Homophones are also called **sound-a-likes**.

- **Same** pronunciation
- **Different** spelling
- **Different** meanings

Homophones are called **sound-a-likes**.

Examples:

- Lola's <u>son</u> is handsome.

    Noun: a male child

- The <u>sun</u> blinded my eyes.

    Noun: a hot, heavenly star

Examples of Homophones

1. **scent:** a smell   **cent:**   one penny
2. **too:** excessive   **two:**   a numeral
3. **council:** a group of people   **counsel:**   to give advice
4. **morning:** early time of day   **mourning:** grieving a loss
5. **birth:**   giving life   **berth:** space
6. **profit:**   extra money   **prophet:** a divinely inspired teacher

What is a Homograph?

Homographs are words that share the same spelling, different pronunciation and different meanings.

- **Same** spelling
- **Different** pronunciation
- **Different** meanings

Examples:

- <u>Dove</u>

    Noun: a bird
- <u>Dove</u>

    Verb: to move downward

Examples of Homographs

1. close: to be near	**close:** to shut
2. bow: a decoration	**bow:** to bend
3. record: musical disc	**record:** write down
4. escort: a companion	**escort:** to attend
5. resume: employment summary	**resume:** to continue

Knowledge Check

1. _____ are also called **look-a-likes.**

2. _____ are also called **sound-a-likes**.

3. _____ share the same spelling, different pronunciation and different meanings.

Answers at bottom of page.

1. Homonyms 2. homophones 3. homographs

EXERCISE 1
Homonyms & Homophones

Directions: Search the following sentences for homonym (**look–a–like**) and homophone (**sound-a–like**) errors. **Cross out** the incorrect word and **insert** the correct spelling.

1. Armand doesn't mind that he was past over for a promotion; he plans to except a new position at the end of the month.

2. Weather or not it rains, we're going to the performance at the outdoor theater.

3. Do you no who's jacket this is? Its not mine and it's not your's.

4. Accept for Julio, everyone here has been to Miami.

5. They are supposed to sit in the last row because there late.

6. The Jacksons have razed ten foster children over the years; that's quite a family.

7. Before she new what she was doing, Annice had walked a block passed the bus stop.

8. If you're going buy the sports shop, please pick up too pairs of goggles.

9. Joel hoped that his knew job on Sundays would not effect his grade-point average.

10. Myako is more used to this whether than Joyce is.

Answers on pages 155.

EXERCISE 2
Homonyms & Homophones

Directions: Search the following sentences for homonym (**look-a–like**) and homophone (**sound-a–like**) errors. **Cross out** the incorrect word and **insert** the correct spelling.

1. I hope you're just being cute when you tale me that my suitcase is missing.

2. The morning star seemed to loose some of it's brilliance.

3. Please put your books they're on the table.

4. A chill came over my hole body.

5. Jingling the lose change in his pockets, Jim said, "So whose going to treat me to the movies?"

6. Although the old saying claims that know knews is good news, I love listening to the news.

7. Marci has trouble excepting compliments; she blushes and becomes quiet.

8. What effect will the strike have on the sell of hot dogs?

9. You have something serious on your mined.

10. Hughes left all his money to his air.

Answers on pages 156.

EXERCISE 3
Homonyms & Homophones

> **Directions:** Search the following sentences for homonym (**look-a–like**) and homophone (**sound-a–like**) errors. **Circle the correct word.**

1. When writing a research paper, you must first (**cite, site**) your sources.

2. Thomas (**ate, eight**) too much food.

3. A bird (**flu, flew**) into the grocery store and scared several customers.

4. Dennis did not (**know, no**) the answer to the question the professor asked.

5. Tamika learned her multiplication tables by (**rote, wrote**).

6. My parents gave us (**they're, their**) old furniture.

7. Kevin waited (**too, two**) whole hours for his date to get dressed.

8. Time passes slowly in a prison (**sell, cell**).

9. Getting a driver's license is a (**right, rite**) of passage for American teens.

10. Prince Charles is (**heir, err**) to the throne.

Answers on pages 156.

Chapter 10

SYNONYMS & ANTONYMS

What is a Synonym?

Synonyms have the **same or similar meaning** as another word.

Example:

- **Silly** can also mean **foolish.**

Word
- sufficient
- enormous
- difficult
- anxious

Synonym
- enough
- huge
- challenging
- worried

To find another word that is the same or similar to a word that you are looking up, use a **thesaurus** or a dictionary.

What is an Antonym?

Antonyms have the **opposite meaning** as another word.

Example:

- **Selfish** means the **opposite** of **generous.**

Word
- tall
- hot
- expensive
- arrogant

Antonym
- short
- cold
- cheap
- humble

EXERCISE 1
Synonyms

Directions: Choose the correct **synonym** for the underlined word.

1. **adequate** light
   a. bright
   b. sufficient
   c. additional

2. Very **reluctant**
   a. happy
   b. delicious
   c. unwilling

3. **Preliminary** decision
   a. best
   b. first
   c. last

4. A great **challenge**
   a. test
   b. meaning
   c. lie

5. To **deceive** someone
   a. leave
   b. steal from
   c. trick

6. Feel **fatigued**
   a. heavy
   b. tired
   c. rested

7. **Cautious** attitude
   a. silly
   b. careless
   c. careful

8. **Preceding** page
   a. after
   b. before
   c. later

9. **accomplish** a task
   a. deny
   b. complete
   c. shirk

10. A **majority** vote
    a. greater part
    b. lesser part
    c. equal part

Answers on page 157.

EXERCISE 2
Synonyms

Directions: Choose the correct **synonym** for the underlined word.

1. **Recommendation**

   a. announcement
   b. suggestion
   c. compliment

2. **Beverage**

   a. food
   b. liquid
   c. drink

3. **Steady**

   a. unreliable
   b. complete
   c. constant

4. **Contemplate**

   a. think
   b. learn
   c. study

5. **Mix**

   a. roll
   b. blend
   c. vibrate

6. **Teach**

   a. learn
   b. educate
   c. study

7. **Immature**

   a. retired
   b. smart
   c. young

8. **Mistake**

   a. error
   b. omission
   c. sentence

9. **Enthusiasm**

   a. will
   b. goal
   c. passion

10. **Shout**

    a. yell
    b. say
    c. speak

Answers on page 157.

EXERCISE 3
Antonyms

Directions: Choose the correct **antonym** for the underlined word.

1. **Seize** the suspect

   a. grab
   b. grip
   c. release

2. A big **promotion**

   a. demotion
   b. upgrade
   c. advancement

3. **Interesting** speaker

   a. charming
   b. boring
   c. knowledgeable

4. **Humid** weather

   a. windy
   b. warm
   c. dry

5. **Master** of the castle

   a. owner
   b. tenant
   c. servant

6. **Genuine** leather

   a. fake
   b. real
   c. natural

7. **Mark** the answer

   a. write
   b. erase
   c. draw

8. **General** information

   a. unlimited
   b. common
   c. specific

9. **Former** president

   a. current
   b. previous
   c. deceased

10. **Faulty** brakes

   a. flawed
   b. unfit
   c. functioning

Answers on page 157.

EXERCISE 4
Antonyms

Directions: Choose the correct **antonym** for the underlined word.

1. **Special**

   a. ordinary
   b. popular
   c. cool

2. **Sober**

   a. intoxicated
   b. complicated
   c. reliable

3. **Extend**

   a. include
   b. retract
   c. remove

4. **Shrink**

   a. limit
   b. produce
   c. expand

5. **Alert**

   a. calm
   b. sleepy
   c. passionate

6. **Fiction**

   a. fable
   b. story
   c. fact

7. **Shiny**

   a. dull
   b. dark
   c. rich

8. **Reckless**

   a. fast
   b. careful
   c. lazy

9. **Quickly**

   a. hastily
   b. slowly
   c. rapidly

10. **Sadly**

   a. angrily
   b. gladly
   c. fearfully

Answers on page 157.

Chapter 11

PUNCTUATION

Punctuation Essentials

In today's digital world of text messages, abbreviations and emoticons, punctuation is often omitted from sentences. However, punctuation marks are essential to comprehending messages according to the writer's original intentions. Despite arguments to the contrary, effective punctuation usage is still important to good sentence construction. These rules are based on *The Gregg Reference Manual* for business writing.

Apostrophe

Singular Possession:	Examples:
Use an **apostrophe** to show **possession** or ownership (singular).	• **Sharon's** loft
	• **Women's** department
	• **Grant's** briefcase
Add an **apostrophe** ('s) to nouns that do not already end with the letter *"s"*.	
Plural Possession:	Examples:
Use an **apostrophe** (s') to show **possession** or plural ownership.	• A **guys'** night out
	• The **twins'** room
Add an apostrophe (s') to plural nouns **after** the final **"s"**.	• The **teachers'** lounge
Contractions:	Examples:
Use an **apostrophe** where one or more **letters** have been omitted.	• I **can't** attend your performance tonight.
• **can't** (cannot) • **it's** (it is)	• **It's** not easy to create a social media marketing plan.
Numbers:	Examples:
Use an **apostrophe** where one or more **numbers** have been omitted.	• Class of **'89** (1989)
	• Summer of **'99** (1999)
**Some style guides support omitting the apostrophe, but most add it for the sake of clarity.	• the **1990's** (1990s)**
	• the **80's** (80s) **

Colon Usage

Lists (Numbered or Bulleted):	**Examples:**
Use a **colon** to introduce lists. A **complete sentence** must **precede** or come before the listed items.	• **The following cities were represented at regionals:** Dallas, Atlanta, Memphis, and New Orleans.
Insert a **colon** before these **signal phrases** that introduce a list: *for example, namely, the following,* or *as follows.*	• **Please buy the following items from the office supply store:** 1. paper clips 2. file folders 3. sticky notes
Clock Time:	**Examples:**
Use a **colon** to separate **hours** and **minutes** in time related phrases.	• 7:15 a.m. • 1:30 p.m. • 11:11 a.m.
Ratios:	**Examples:**
Use a **colon** to express **ratios**.	• **4:1** ratio of single women to men • **5:1** betting odds

Comma Rules

Rule #1:	**Example:**
Use a comma to separate a series of three or more items: nouns, verbs or adjectives.	• Tim arrived at the airport, waited in line, checked his baggage, **and** walked down the concourse to the plane.
Rule #2:	**Example (No Oxford Comma):**
In a list of items, putting a **comma** before the conjunction **"and"** is *technically* optional.	• Sheila placed the order for magazines, newspapers **and** cookbooks.
The optional comma before the word "and" within a series or list of items is called the **Oxford comma**, which is used for the sake of clarity. Either way is correct.	**Example (Oxford Comma):** • Sheila placed the order for magazines, newspapers, **and** cookbooks.

Rule #3:	Examples:
Use a **comma** after an **introductory word**, **phrase** or **dependent** clause. **Clauses** can appear at the **beginning** or **end** of a sentence.	• **Before you call,** send a text. • Martin only needed one thing, **confidence.**

Rule #4:	Example:
Use a **comma** after the **day** and **calendar year** when citing a full date that include the month, day and year.	• Ahnna will arrive on **September 9, 2018,** for the training session.

Rule #5:	Examples:
Use a **comma** to separate **two** or **more adjectives** that describe a noun.	• The applicant was **professional, knowledgeable,** and **experienced** in the area of accounting.

Rule #6:	Examples:
Use **commas** to enclose parenthetical words, phrases or clauses, especially appositives. **Appositives** rename or give more detail about the subject, such as in the second example, *"our chapter president."*	• The additional supply order, **however,** will not ship until early tomorrow. • Ms. Mel Temple, **our chapter president,** will speak now.

Rule #7:	Examples:
Use a **comma** before the word **"not"** to express a negative thought, opinion or circumstance.	• I want mustard, **not mayonnaise,** on my burger. • Terence sets the security code at closing, **not Melanie.**

Rule #8:	Examples:
Use a **comma** after an **adverb** that comes at the beginning of a sentence.	• **Finally,** I can get some work done. • **Actually,** you cannot get paid for working overtime on the weekend.

Rule #9:	Examples:
Put a **comma** after the words **"Yes"** or **"No"** when they begin a sentence.	• **Yes,** I love turkey sandwiches. • **No,** I did not edit the annual report; Adam did.

Rule #10:	Examples:
Use **commas** to separate parts of a **mailing address,** especially the **city** and **state.**	• Send the check to 171 State St., **Dallas, Texas** 89332.

Rule #11:	Examples:
Use **commas** to separate dates from the rest of a sentence.	• **June 25, 2009,** was a sad day for Michael Jackson fans. • **Thursday, June 25, 2009,** was a sad day for Michael Jackson fans. • **June 25, 2009,** was a sad day for Michael Jackson fans.
Rule #12: Use **commas** in **numbers** larger than **999**.	Examples: • The company paid **$27,325** for computer upgrades last year. • Give us **1,000** bottles of spring water for the race this Saturday.

Diagonal/Slash

Use **diagonals** in **abbreviations** and expressions of **time**.	Examples:
	
	   • c/o (care of)
	   • b/s (bill of sale)
	   • w/ (with)
	   • 24/7

Use **slashes** to express alternatives.	Examples:
	
	   • on/off switch
	   • AM/FM

Use **diagonals** to express **two** **functions** or components.	Examples:
	
	   • owner/manager
	   • client/server network

Use **slashes** to write fractions.
 	
** **Do not** leave a space before or after the slash, also called a *virgule*.
	Examples:
	
	   • 2/3 of the votes
	   • 1/2 of the audience

Ellipsis

Use the **ellipsis** to indicate **missing words** from a quotation.	**Examples:** • "Darkness cannot drive out darkness. . ." said Dr. Martin Luther King, Jr.
Use the **ellipsis** to express **thoughts** that trail off.	• "You took the money, closed the account and. . .?"
Use the **ellipsis** to express a deliberate pause or to *throw shade*.	• My art show is tonight. Bring a friend. . .if you have one.

Em Dash (Dash)

Em dashes set off single words or phrases to show special emphasis.	**Examples:** • Zumba—that's what he lives for every Saturday morning. • **Power, money, fame**—these were her aspirations in life.
Em dashes set off a series.	**Example:** • **The winners—Allen, Stacey and Danny—**have entered the finals.
Em dashes indicate a sudden interruption in thought or a break in sentence structure.	**Example:** • The title—**if it has a title**—is missing from the page.
Em dashes precede the words *these*, *they* and *all* when summarizing a list of details.	**Examples:** • Radio, magazines, and newspapers—**these** will suffer major advertising losses. • Tina, Mark, and Bethany—**they** all won scholarships. • **Arkansas, Texas, Louisiana**—all are important markets for new business.

En Dash (Hyphen)

Use **hyphens** to show a range of numbers. Remember, hyphens are shorter than em dashes.	**Examples:** • 1997-2001 • 8:00 a.m.-5:00 p.m. • pp. 11-40
Use **hyphens** to indicate the life span of someone who is still alive.	**Examples:** • President Bill Clinton (**1946-**) • Beyoncé Giselle Carter (**1981-**)
Use **hyphens** to indicate a period of time that spans two back-to-back calendar years.	**Examples:** • Spring **2017-2018** • Fiscal year **2000-2001**
Hyphenate numbers from **21 to 99**.	**Examples:** • Chris bought **thirty-two** assorted bags of candy for Halloween. • Tammy owes four hundred and **ninety-six** dollars in late tax fees.
Use **hyphens** to express **compound words** or **adjectives**.	**Examples:** • **Hot-water** bottle • **Make-up** brushes • **Half-chocolate-half-vanilla**
Use **hyphens** in **telephone numbers**.	**Examples:** • 888-777-9311 • (282) 541-1908 • 1-800-FLOWERS
Use **hyphens** for **ages** acting as adjectives or nouns.	**Examples:** • 100-year-old house (adjective) • A bunch of 3-year-olds (noun)

Exclamation Point

Use **exclamation points** to end sentences that express strong emotion.	**Examples:** • **Stop!** The light is red! • What a great room!

Use **exclamation points** instead of a question mark to express strong emotion.	**Examples:** • What did I tell you! • How could you do that!
Use **exclamation points** after single words to express enthusiasm, surprise, disbelief or intense emotion.	**Examples:** • **Congratulations!** You won! • **Yes!** I'm engaged! • **Oh!** I didn't expect that!
Use **exclamation points** after **repeated words** that are used for emphasis.	**Example:** • **Going! Going!** Our sale is almost over!

Italics

Main Titles and Subtitles Italicize the **main title** AND the **subtitle** of full-length, **published** books, and other creative compositions.	**Examples:** • *Revolting Bodies: The Struggle to Redefine Fat Identity* • *Can I Get a Witness?: Black Women and Depression* • *Desire: The Journey We Must Take to Find the Life God Offers*
Creative Works: Italicize the names of full-length, **published** creative, literary, periodical, and musical compositions when citing them within sentences.	**Examples:** • **Books:** *The Bluest Eye* • **Magazines:** *Newsweek* • **Newspapers:** *USA Today*

Parentheses

Use **parentheses** to enclose (nonessential) information that relates to its surrounding text.	**Examples:** • The illustration (**see page 94**) is very important.
Parentheses signal **"by the way"** to the reader.	• Marion doesn't feel (**and why should he**) like teaching the disruptive class.

Period

Sentences	Examples:
Always end a **complete sentence** with a period.	• Gary ironed his suit**.** • Oliver fed his newborn daughter and fell asleep**.**
Numbers	Examples:
Use **periods** as **decimal points** in numerical expressions.	• **88.5** degrees • **$15.95** per unit
Inside Parentheses	Examples:
If the phrase inside the **parenthesis** is a complete sentence **(independent clause),** put the period **inside** the parenthesis.	• Tammy feels woozy. **(Her head hurts.)** • Soup is on sale. **(Chicken noodle is the best flavor.)**
Outside Parentheses	Example:
If the phrase inside the **parenthesis** is **NOT** a complete sentence, put the period **outside** the parenthesis.	• Tammy felt some strange symptoms yesterday **(dizziness and shoulder pains).**

Question Mark

Question marks end sentences written as questions or inquiries.	Examples:
	• Where are my glasses? • Did you pack your shoes? Your socks?

Quotation Mark

Dialogue	Example:
Use **quotation marks** to indicate **direct quotes** or dialogue.	• Manuel asked the interviewer, **"What is the starting salary?"**
Titles of Creative Works: Use **quotation marks** to indicate **titles** of short works: speeches, sermons, magazines, essays, plays, films, brochures, songs, poems, articles, chapters, reports, events, lectures, or unpublished works.	Example: • Have you read my speech **"The Power of Reputation?"** • The poem **"Now"** by Audre Lorde is short and powerful.

With Punctuation	Examples:
Periods and **commas** are placed **inside** the closing quotation marks.	• "I wanted," Lucetta said, "to finish this meeting on time."
Colons and **semicolons** are placed **outside** closing quotation marks.	• The following animals are considered **"marsupials"**: kangaroo, koala, and opossum.
Question marks and **exclamation points** can appear **inside** or **outside** closing quotation marks.	• "How are you?!" Betty yelled. • Have you read the report, **"Successful Start-up Businesses"**?

Semicolon

Use a **semicolon** to connect two **independent clauses (complete sentences)** that are related in meaning, but not joined by a conjunction.	Examples: • Operations tripled productivity in the first **quarter;** marketing doubled in revenue. • Margarine costs less than **butter;** it contains less saturated fat.
Use a **semicolon** in a **list** of items that contain commas. The **semicolon** separates each individual item to reduce confusion.	Example: • The officers of the school board are John Robinson, President; Susan Tate, Vice-President; Becky Feeny, Treasurer; James Jackson, Secretary; and Jan Jenkins, Historian.
Use a **semicolon** when joining **two independent clauses** with transitional expressions such as: • consequently • however • nevertheless • therefore	Example: • Ruth dealt with difficult customers effectively; **consequently,** we forwarded all the tough calls to her extension.

EXERCISE 1
Commas

Directions: Choose the sentence in which all the commas are used correctly. Circle the correct answer.

1. a. At the dance school, we learned to waltz, to merengue, and to line dance on Saturday.
   b. At the dance school we learned, to waltz, to merengue and to line dance on Saturday.
   c. At the dance school, we learned to waltz, to merengue on and, to line dance on Saturday.

2. a. Because I did not know that Jackie, my roommate from college, was coming to visit me I went to Columbia South Carolina for the weekend.
   b. Because I did not know that Jackie, my roommate from college, was coming to visit me, I went to Columbia, South Carolina, for the weekend.
   c. Because I did not know that Jackie my roommate from college was coming to visit me, I went to Columbia, South Carolina for the weekend.

3. a. The 1985 Ford which has ignition trouble is hard to start.
   b. The 1985 Ford, which has ignition trouble is hard to start.
   c. The 1985 Ford, which has ignition trouble, is hard to start.

4. a. On Saturday, August 5, 1986, Saks' men's department sold more polo shirts, Izod sweaters, and canvas belts than it had in three months.
   b. On Saturday, August 5, 1986, Saks' men's department sold more polo shirts, Izod sweaters and canvas belts than it had in three months.
   c. On Saturday August 5, 1986, Saks' men's department sold more polo shirts Izod sweaters, and canvas belts than it had in three months.

5. a. Your plan for a day-care center by the way, is the best I have ever seen.
   b. Your plan for a day-care center, by the way is the best I have ever seen.
   c. Your plan for a day-care center, by the way, is the best I have ever seen.

Answers on page 158

EXERCISE 2

Punctuation

Directions: Insert the correct punctuation for each sentence below. Some sentences require more than one punctuation mark.

1. Are we there yet she asked

2. Everyones going to Sashas for dinner at eight.

3. Mix the oil and vinegar at a 1 2 ratio.

4. I hope I get a lot of presents today is my birthday.

5. Stop talking to me

6. My little sister is 10 years old

7. By the way your dad called about an hour ago.

8. Ayanna my supervisor was born September 9 1981.

9. You need these items for the cookie recipe salt sugar and flour.

10. Mr. Stackhouses daughter is wearing earbuds and cant hear you.

Answers on page 158.

Practical Grammar Essentials

POST-TEST

Congratulations on completing the exercises in this book! Now that you have absorbed a great deal of grammar knowledge, let's see how much you have learned.

1. Channel 30 specialized _____ shows for campers and hunters.

   a. in
   b. on
   c. for

2. The more Gerald worries _____ the work he has left to do, the less able he is to finish on time.

   a. about
   b. after
   c. on

3. Neither Jack nor Bill remembered to bring _____ membership card to the gym.

   a. they're
   b. their
   c. his

4. The University Judiciary Board, composed of twelve undergraduate students, reached _____ decision on the date rape case.

   a. their
   b. our
   c. its

5. Tim laughed when he saw the way that_____ had dressed for the Halloween party.
   a. Serena and I
   b. Serena and me

6. When Jamal came looking for_____, we had already left.

   a. Karen and I
   b. Karen and me

7. Families **(travels, travel)** most frequently during the holidays.

8. Recess **(provides, provide)** important opportunities for children to develop physically.

9. Most people taste their food first, they salt it later.

        a.   comma splice

        b.   run-on

10. Keith set up a new website it combined creativity with ease of use.

        a.   comma splice

        b.   run-on

11. When the manager called me this morning.

        a.   fragment

        b.   correct

12. Hand me the newspaper.

        a.   fragment

        b.   correct

13. The weather is terrible many holiday parties have been cancelled.

        a.   fragment

        b.   run-on

14. Mr. Williams will not attend the meeting, his department will not attend the conference.

        a.   comma splice

        b.   run-on

15. **Cross out the prepositional phrase(s):**

The cars on the showroom floor are new.

16. **Cross out the prepositional phrase(s):**

The reasons for my call are difficult to explain quickly.

17. **Cross out the prepositional phrase(s):**

Colleen, in addition to her two cousins, starts college in August.

18. Stuck under his chair, Paul felt a large blob of bubble gum.

        a.   Dangling Modifier
        b.   Misplaced Modifier

19. Typing the last document, the computers in the library crashed.

        a.   Dangling Modifier
        b.   Misplaced Modifier

20. The beautiful woman walked into the charity ball with her husband wearing her newest designer dress.

        a.   Dangling Modifier
        b.   Misplaced Modifier

Questions 21-25: Choose the **best** version of each sentence below.

21. a. Sizzling over an open flame, the smell of Zack's burgers made the guests hungry.
    b. Sizzling over an open flame, Zack's guests eagerly awaited the aromatic burgers.
    c. Sizzling over an open flame, Zack's burgers smelled delicious and made his guests hungry.

22. a. Allison made nearly two thousand dollars over the summer.
    b. Allison nearly made two thousand dollars over the summer.
    c. Nearly, Allison made two thousand dollars over the summer.

23. a. Working as a team, the job was completed quickly.
    b. The job was completed quickly working as a team.
    c. Working as a team, Orlando and Jamal completed the job quickly.

24. a. There was nothing on television Joshua decided to wash his car.
    b. There was nothing on television, therefore, Joshua decided to wash his car.
    c. There was nothing on television, so Joshua decided to wash his car.

25. a. Melody says her parents gave her the right name. Because she loves to sing, play the piano, and listen to music.
    b. Melody says her parents gave her the right name, because she loves to sing, play the piano, and listen to music.
    c. Melody says her parents. Gave her the right name. Because she loves to sing, play the piano, and listen to music.

Answers on next page.

POST-TEST ANSWERS

1. a
2. a
3. c
4. c
5. a
6. b
7. travel
8. provides
9. a
10. b
11. a
12. b
13. b
14. a
15. on the showroom floor
16. for my call
17. in addition to her cousins; **in August**
18. b
19. a
20. a
21. c
22. a
23. c
24. c
25. b

CHAPTER 1 ANSWERS

EXERCISE 1: Grammar Terms

1. Noun	6. Conjunction
2. Adverb	7. Article
3. Pronoun	8. Interjection
4. Verb	9. Preposition
5. Pronoun	10. Object (Direct)

EXERCISE 2: Grammar Terms

1. Adjective	6. Pronoun
2. Verb (Linking)	7. Verb
3. Noun	8. Interjection
4. Adverb	9. Article
5. Conjunction	10. Preposition

EXERCISE 3: Grammar Terms

1. Verb	6. Preposition
2. Noun (Obj. of Prep)	7. Adjective
3. Adjective	8. Verb
4. Adverb	9. Noun
5. Pronoun	10. Preposition

EXERCISE 4: Articles

1. a	6. an
2. the	7. a
3. a	8. a
4. an	9. the
5. the	10. the

CHAPTER 2 ANSWERS

EXERCISE 1: Types of Sentences

1. Simple
2. Complex
3. Compound
4. Simple
5. Compound-Complex

6. Compound-Complex
7. Simple
8. Compound
9. Compound
10. Complex

EXERCISE 2: Identifying Clauses

1. Peter was a disciple **who denied Jesus three times**.
2. The NAACP, **which was founded in 1910**, accomplished a great deal in the struggle for civil rights.
3. Presidential candidates must strike **while the iron is hot**.
4. **If wishes were horses**, beggars would ride.
5. **Since Mr. Johns, the best principal in the district, retired**, many teachers do not feel secure or supported in their classrooms.
6. Jesse and Jeremy always get into trouble **whenever their cousin Rob comes to town**.
7. **When planning a garden**, you must consider the annual temperature range in your area.
8. Mozart, **who was a musical genius and a child prodigy,** died young.
9. **Because love is not a requirement for marriage**, many marriages end in divorce.
10. **After lunch is served**, students prepare for recess.

EXERCISE 3: Identifying Subjects

1. the school district
2. heavy rains
3. Jane
4. Todd
5. You (Understood)

6. Craig and Karen
7. Ahnna and her co-workers
8. Kevin and Kandis
9. You (Understood)
10. the trees

EXERCISE 4: Subjects and Predicates

1. (You) should bring a change of clothes to the beach.

2. (Shanda) always stretches before going on her daily run.

3. A (box) of cookies is in the cupboard behind the peanut butter.
4. (One) of Josephine's contact lenses fell out of her eye.
5. A mystery (admirer) from Ian's office sent a bouquet of flowers.
6. (I) should have taken more writing courses before going to graduate school.

7. (Miguel) can tell the difference between a male and a female parrot.
8. (Bram Stoker) is best known for his novel, *Dracula*.

9. Your (tickets) will be sent to you by the first week of November.

10. (One) of our subscribers wrote a letter of complaint about the magazine.

CHAPTER 3 ANSWERS

EXERCISE 1: Sentence Fragments

1.	b	6.	b
2.	a	7.	a
3.	b	8.	a
4.	a	9.	b
5.	b	10.	b

EXERCISE 2: Sentence Fragments

1.	a	6.	a
2.	b	7.	b
3.	a	8.	a
4.	a	9.	b
5.	b	10.	a

EXERCISE 3: Sentence Fragments

1. Fragment	6. Complete
2. Complete	7. Fragment
3. Fragment	8. Complete
4. Complete	9. Fragment
5. Fragment	10. Complete

EXERCISE 4: Sentence Fragments

1. At the end of the business day, it is crucial for all employees to follow proper closing procedures for the breakroom. **Before you leave**. Make sure to wash all dirty dishes. **And empty the trash of smelly food containers**. The cleaning crew will trash everything left in the refrigerators at 5 p.m. every Friday.

2. **Finding time for yourself**. **Is an important part of a healthy lifestyle**. You may be neglecting your own physical and spiritual needs. **If you are constantly focused on caring for other people**. Research shows that people who set aside time to relax and enjoy life are actually better friends, co-workers and spouses. **Than those who spend all their time accommodating others**.

3. Getting a great deal on a flight for your next vacation is possible. **If you can plan ahead and search several travel and airline websites**. Buying 21 days in advance can save you a great deal of money. Also, try to fly after 7:00 p.m. Finally, shop around.

4. We are pleased to announce that Tireshia Davis is November's employee of the month. **Meeting all company goals and a good team player**. She will receive a $100 gift certificate to *Bed Bath & Beyond*. Please join us in congratulating Tireshia. **When you see her around the office**. Show your appreciation for her contributions to this department.

CHAPTER 4 ANSWERS

EXERCISE 1: Run-on Sentences

1. **RUN-ON:** The chocolate chips can be melted in the microwave; the eggs can be added one at a time in the bowl.
2. **CORRECT**: David's cat cringed at the sight of the can of flea powder.
3. **CORRECT**: Deer roamed the wooded area long before developers built homes there.
4. **RUN-ON:** Shop once a week; stick to a preplanned grocery list.
5. **CORRECT**: Admitting to cheating on his girlfriend was honestly difficult for Marco.
6. **RUN-ON:** Marnie loves scary movies. Tony, her boyfriend, refuses to watch them.
7. **CORRECT**: Dorothy Woods won the Business Woman of the Year award from the Junior League.
8. **RUN-ON:** Your buttermilk biscuits taste superb; they are the best I've ever eaten.
9. **CORRECT**: D'Andre applied for a small business loan to open a barbershop.
10. **RUN-ON:** Margarine costs less than butter; it contains less saturated fat.

EXERCISE 2: Run-on Sentences

1. **RUN-ON:** The magazine sells for seventy-five cents**. In Canada,** it costs eighty cents.
2. **CORRECT:** Clouds of smoke filling the train cabins frightened the passengers.
3. **RUN-ON:** The singer included several unannounced songs**. In the live show,** she changed the program.
4. **RUN-ON:** They taught the parrot how to speak**;** its words were indistinguishable.
5. **RUN-ON:** Search carefully for grandma's old recipe book**. There** are several places in the attic to look.
6. **CORRECT:** Using real butter is the key to baking great potato skins.
7. **CORRECT:** Concert pianists must practice six to eight hours a day.
8. **RUN-ON:** Hot dogs are a typical American food**.** Mrs. Roosevelt served them in the White House.
9. **CORRECT:** My cat sleeps on her special blanket every night.
10. **CORRECT:** A butterfly's wings are too large for efficient flying.

EXERCISE 3: Comma Splices

1. Comma Splice - a
2. Comma Splice - a
3. Correct - b
4. Comma Splice - a
5. Correct - b
6. Correct - b
7. Comma Splice - a
8. Comma Splice - a
9. Correct - b
10. Correct - b

EXERCISE 4: Run-ons & Comma Splices

1. **RUN-ON:** Concussions are a huge problem in football**;** too many players are suffering.
2. **COMMA SPLICE:** Tell your visitors not to park in front of the building**;** their cars will be towed.
3. **CORRECT:** My father does not watch football. He does not enjoy sports.
4. **COMMA SPLICE:** Dell's band will open for Boney James in Memphis and in Little Rock**. He** will travel alone to the show in Dallas.
5. **CORRECT:** Marsha started a blog for natural health, but her writing is terrible.
6. **RUN-ON:** People who take Zumba classes are much happier than those who cycle**. No** research supports these statements, just my personal opinion.
7. **COMMA SPLICE:** Tiffany applied for an executive assistant position**. The** interviewer said her name sounded too young for the seasoned staff on the job.
8. **RUN-ON:** Nathan changed his status to "in a relationship" on Facebook**. He** received   many likes.
9. **RUN-ON:** Evelyn over sang her original song at the gospel festival, so the DJ cut the music early**. She** continued to sing a capella, until the host took the stage.
10. **COMMA SPLICE:** Friends come**;** friends go. Such is life.

CHAPTER 5 ANSWERS

EXERCISE 1: Prepositions

1. Roslyn became a successful corporate accountant ~~in spite of her traumatic childhood~~.

2. Perry always meditates ~~before writing a sermon~~.

3. Braylon hid his favorite cookies ~~behind the microwave~~.

4. One of Carla's extensions fell out ~~of her hair during our cardio kick boxing class~~.

5. A generous client sent Stephen an expensive bottle ~~of wine for landing a huge contract~~.

6. Nina should have checked the weather reports ~~before washing her car~~.

7. Many bank tellers cannot tell the difference ~~between a fake $100 bill and a real one~~.

8. Alice Walker is best known ~~for her novel *The Color Purple*~~.

9. Your first direct deposit should post ~~by the last Friday of this month~~.

10. ~~Since her car stopped running a few days ago~~, Rhonda has not left the house.

EXERCISE 2: Prepositions

1. (Jamarion) **bought** the jogging suit ~~with blue pinstripes~~.

2. (I) **missed** my bus more often ~~than not last month~~.

3. The new computer (course) **was filled** ~~with students by the first hour of registration~~.

4. The (job) **was** a good opportunity ~~for Orlando to learn about merchandising~~.

5. The (Arkansas Razorbacks) **were thrilled** ~~with their triple overtime victory~~.

6. (Two) ~~of my neighbors~~ **have been feuding** ~~over parking spaces for weeks~~.

7. ~~In the course of three days~~, forest (fires) **destroyed** most ~~of the national park~~.

8. Two-paycheck (families) **are becoming** less common ~~in this crazy economy~~.

9. ~~For a skilled tailor~~, (sewing) a skirt **presents** no problem.

10. The (Million Man March) **changed** the lives ~~of millions of people~~.

EXERCISE 3: Prepositions

1.	a	6.	a
2.	b	7.	a
3.	a	8.	b
4.	b	9.	b
5.	a	10.	b

CHAPTER 6 ANSWERS

EXERCISE 1: Subject-Verb Agreement

1.	has	- a	6.	lives	- b
2.	goes, get	- b	7.	chases	- b
3.	is	- b	8.	tastes	- b
4.	impresses	- b	9.	agrees	- b
5.	is	- a	10.	runs	- a

EXERCISE 2: Subject-Verb Agreement

1.	is	6.	plans
2.	use	7.	follow
3.	are	8.	are
4.	gives	9.	pinpoint
5.	are	10.	frustrates

EXERCISE 3: Subject-Verb Agreement

1.	wants	6.	are
2.	stop	7.	offer
3.	check	8.	interfere
4.	provides	9.	looks
5.	furnish	10.	jogs

EXERCISE 4: Subject-Verb Agreement

1.	is	6.	shows
2.	is	7.	extends
3.	needs	8.	is
4.	has	9.	has agreed
5.	was	10.	was

CHAPTER 7 ANSWERS

EXERCISE 1: Noun-Pronoun Agreement

1. c
2. a
3. c
4. b
5. c

6. a
7. c
8. a
9. b
10. c

EXERCISE 2: Noun-Pronoun Agreement

1. her
2. its
3. her
4. his
5. He

6. The voicemail greeting
7. She
8. I
9. whom
10. I

EXERCISE 3: Noun-Pronoun Agreement

1. they
2. his or her
3. their
4. their
5. their

6. they
7. her
8. his or her
9. their
10. her

CHAPTER 8 ANSWERS

EXERCISE 1: Dangling & Misplaced Modifiers

1. C
2. DM
3. DM
4. C
5. DM

6. C
7. DM
8. C
9. C
10. C

EXERCISE 2: Dangling & Misplaced Modifiers
(Suggested Answers)

1. Plump sausages, the dinner guests looked forward to the main course.

- **The dinner guests looked forward to the main course, <u>plump sausages.</u>**

- **Explanation:** Move the <u>**misplaced modifier**</u> near the thing it describes or modifies: **the main course**.

2. Soaring over the treetops in a hot air balloon, the view was spectacular.

    - **Soaring over the treetops in a hot air balloon, <u>the couple</u> enjoyed the spectacular view.**

    - **Explanation:** Add a subject to this **<u>dangling modifier</u>**. Who soars over the treetops in a hot air balloon?

3. Powered by hydrogen, the engineers designed a new kind of car.

    - **The engineers designed a new kind of car <u>powered by hydrogen</u>.**

    - **Explanation:** Move the **<u>misplaced modifier</u>** near the thing it describes or modifies: **a new kind of car**.

4. I introduced my boyfriend to my father, who wanted to marry me.

    - **I introduced my boyfriend, <u>who wanted to marry me</u>, to my father.**

    - **Explanation:** Move the **<u>misplaced modifier</u>** near the thing it describes or modifies: **boyfriend.**

5. Revised to highlight his computer expertise, Marcelo was proud of his new resumé.

    - **Marcelo was proud of his new resumé, <u>revised to highlight his computer expertise</u>.**
                        OR

    - **Marcelo was proud of his new resumé, <u>which he revised to highlight his computer expertise</u>.**

    - **Explanation:** Move the **<u>misplaced modifier</u>** near the thing it describes or modifies: **resumé.**

6. Jim, who loved to lick car windows, drove his dog to the vet.

    - **Jim drove his dog, <u>who loved to lick car windows</u>, to the vet.**

    - **Explanation:** Move the **<u>misplaced modifier</u>** near the thing it describes or modifies: **dog.**

7. Banging inside the dryer, Carla heard the lost keys.

    - **Carla heard the lost keys <u>banging inside the dryer</u>.**

    - **Explanation:** Move the **<u>misplaced modifier</u>** near the thing it describes or modifies: **lost keys.**

8. We complained about the proposed building to the mayor, which we found ugly and too large for the neighborhood.

- **We complained to the mayor about the proposed building, <u>which we found ugly and too large for the neighborhood.</u>**

- **Explanation:** Move the <u>**misplaced modifier**</u> near the thing it describes or modifies: **the building.**

9. Covered with whipped cream, Brandon carried a chocolate cake.

- **Brandon carried a chocolate cake <u>covered with whipped cream.</u>**

- **Explanation:** Move the <u>**misplaced modifier**</u> near the thing it describes or modifies: **chocolate cake.**

10. A homeless teenager, the nun helped the girl find a place to live.

- **The nun helped the girl, <u>a homeless teenager</u>, find a place to live.**

- **Explanation:** Move the <u>**misplaced modifier**</u> near the thing it describes or modifies: the girl.

EXERCISE 3: Dangling & Misplaced Modifiers
  (Suggested Answers)

1. Slowly cooling off, I took a sip of tea.

- **I took a sip of tea, as it slowly cooled off.**
- **Explanation:** Move this <u>**misplaced modifier**</u> close to "tea," and reword as necessary.

2. Departing on track 12, the commuter anxiously rushed ahead.

- **The commuter anxiously rushed ahead toward the train departing on track 12.**
- **Explanation:** Attaching the <u>**dangling modifier**</u> to a train is a logical connection; trains depart on tracks. Reword the rest of the sentence as necessary for clarity.

3. The weather got worse driving down the interstate.

- **As Sydney drove down the interstate, the weather got worse.**
- **Explanation:** Was the weather driving? Add a person and reword this <u>**dangling modifier**</u> as necessary for clarity.

4. Having received your check, a new bill will be sent out.

- **A new bill will be sent out after we receive your check.**
- Having received your check, **accounting will send out a new bill.**

- **Explanation:** Who will receive the check? What happens next? *Having received your check* is a confusing phrase in this **dangling modifier** that needs to be clarified. Remember, keep the intention of the sentence when rewording.

5. Crying inconsolably, the tears kept flowing long after the movie ended.

   - **As she cried inconsolably, Stephanie's tears** kept flowing long after the movie ended.
   - **Explanation:** Attach a person to this **dangling modifier**, and add a pronoun that agrees.

CHAPTER 9 ANSWERS

EXERCISE 1: Homonyms & Homophones

1. Armand doesn't mind that he was ~~past~~ **passed** over for a promotion; he plans to ~~except~~ **accept** a new position at the end of the month.

2. ~~Weather~~ **Whether** or not it rains, we're going to the performance at the outdoor theater.

3. Do you ~~no who's~~ **know whose** jacket this is? ~~Its~~ **It's** not mine ~~and~~ it's not ~~your's.~~ **yours.**

4. ~~Accept~~ **Except** for Julio, everyone here has been to Miami.

5. They are supposed to sit in the last row because ~~there~~ **they're** late.

6. The Jacksons have ~~razed~~ **raised** ten foster children over the years; that's quite a family.

7. Before she ~~new~~ **knew** what she was doing, Annice had walked a block ~~passed~~ **past** the bus stop.

8. If you're going ~~buy~~ **by** the sports shop, please pick up ~~too~~ **two** pairs of goggles.

9. Joel hoped that his ~~knew~~ **new** job on Sundays would not ~~effect~~ **affect** his grade-point average.

10. Myako is more used to this ~~whether~~ **weather** than Joyce is.

EXERCISE 2: Homonyms & Homophones

1. I hope you're just being cute when you ~~tale~~ *tell* me that my suitcase is missing.

2. The morning star seemed to ~~loose~~ *lose* some of ~~it's~~ *its* brilliance.

3. Please put your books ~~they're~~ *there* on the table.

4. A chill came over my ~~hole~~ *whole* body.

5. Jingling the ~~lose~~ *loose* change in his pockets, Jim said, "So ~~whose~~ *who's* going to treat me to the movies?"

6. Although the old saying claims that ~~know knews~~ *no news* is good news, I love listening to the news.

7. Marci has trouble ~~excepting~~ *accepting* compliments; she blushes and becomes quiet.

8. What effect will the strike have on the ~~sell~~ *sale* of hot dogs?

9. You have something serious on your ~~mined~~ *mind*.

10. Hughes left all his money to his ~~air~~ *heir*.

EXERCISE 3: Homonyms & Homophones

1. cite	6. their
2. ate	7. two
3. flew	8. cell
4. know	9. rite
5. rote	10. heir

CHAPTER 10 ANSWERS

EXERCISE 1: Synonyms

1. b - sufficient
2. c - unwilling
3. b - first
4. a - test
5. c - trick

6. b - tired
7. c - careful
8. b - before
9. b - complete
10. a - greater part

EXERCISE 2: Synonyms

1. b - suggestion
2. c - drink
3. c - constant
4. a - think
5. b - blend

6. b - educate
7. c - young
8. a - error
9. c - passion
10. a - yell

EXERCISE 3: Antonyms

1. c - release
2. a - demotion
3. b - boring
4. c - dry
5. c - servant

6. a - fake
7. b - erase
8. c - specific
9. a - current
10. c - functioning

EXERCISE 4: Antonyms

1. a - ordinary
2. a - intoxicated
3. b - retract
4. c - expand
5. b - sleepy

6. c - fact
7. a - dull
8. b - careful
9. b - slowly
10. b - gladly

CHAPTER 11 ANSWERS

EXERCISE 1: Commas

1. a
2. b
3. c
4. a
5. c

EXERCISE 2: Punctuation

1. **"Are we there yet?"** she asked_._

2. **Everyone's** going to **Sasha's** for dinner at eight.

3. Mix the oil and vinegar at a **1:2** ratio.

4. I hope I get a lot of presents_;_ today is my birthday.
   ~OR~ I hope I get a lot of presents_:_ today is my birthday.

5. Stop talking to me_!_

6. My little sister is 10 years old_._

7. By the way_,_ your dad called about an hour ago.

8. Ayanna_,_ my supervisor_,_ was born September 9_,_ 1981.

9. You need these items for the cookie recipe_:_ salt_,_ sugar_,_ and flour.

   ~OR~ You need these items for the cookie recipe_:_ salt_,_ sugar and flour.

10. Mr. **Stackhouse's** daughter is wearing earbuds and **can't** hear you.

References

Hopper, Vincent F. , Cedric Gale and Benjamin W. Griffith. *Essentials of Writing*. 5th Edition. New York: Barron's Educational Series, Inc., 2000. Print.

Loberger, Gordon and Kate Shoup. *Webster's New World English Grammar Hand Book*. 2nd Edition. New York: Houghton Mifflin Harcourt, 2009. Print.

Peters, Mark. *Idiot's Guide to Grammar and Style*. New York: Alpha/Penguin Publishing Group Inc. (USA), 2014. Print.

Strauss, Jane, Lester K. Kaufman and Tom Stern. *The Blue Book of Grammar and Punctuation*. 11th Edition. California: Jossey-Bass/Wiley, 2014. Print.

New Release 2021

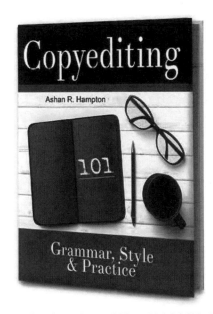

(Full-color) ISBN: 978-1-716-24690-6

"Copyediting 101: Grammar, Style & Practice" is informational and practical. Each chapter provides a succinct understanding of copyediting for a general audience of students, curious learners or experienced proofreaders and writers who want to expand their services. Because this workbook is introductory, anyone with an interest in copyediting and a knack for words can easily engage with the content, which focuses on the grammar, style and usage issues that commonly beleaguer professional and novice writers.

Ordering information:
www.arhampton.com/books

Index

W

Made in United States
North Haven, CT
18 March 2023

34165590R00091